The Quantum Sculler
by James C. Joy
October 2016
2nd Edition

© Copyright 2014, 2016. James C. Joy, The Joy of Sculling.
All rights reserved.

No part of this publication may be reproduced or transmitted in any form or by any means, electronic or mechanical, including photocopying, recording, or any other information storage and retrieval system, without the written permission of the publisher and author.

Published by James C. Joy
ISBN 978-0-9983634-1-7

Post Office Box 567
Geneva, New York 14456

Phone: (315) 781-2383
E-mail: joyofsculling@mac.com
Website: www.thejoyofsculling.com

Cover Design by Haley Sive.

Second Edition Revised and Expanded, October 2016.

Cover photo shows Australian, later Canadian sculler Bobby Pearce of the 1920s and 1930s racing in Vancouver, B.C. He was the gold medal winner in the single sculls at the 1928 Summer Olympics in Amsterdam and the 1932 Summer Olympics in Los Angeles. Pearce won the World Sculling Championship in 1933, a title he defended successfully twice in 1934 and 1938. He was also the 1931 winner of the Diamond Challenge Sculls at Henley Royal Regatta and of the 1928 Gold Cup Challenge in Philadelphia.

Dedication

It is with great passion and pride that I dedicate this book to my spiritual guide, Cecilia Elizabeth Joyce Joy, my companion for 50 years. It has been a wonderful trip through this life with her at my side, serving as a clear illuminating beacon.

The Quantum Sculler

Endorsements

Jimmy,

Thanks again. The Scullers Entry is really a great idea. It's like the difference between classic cross-country and skate cross-country skiing. With classic, your foot stops. With skate, you just keep on accelerating. The Scullers Entry is like rotating the wheel on an upside down bicycle. It doesn't work to grab the wheel and try to speed it up. The only way to speed up the wheel is to contact the wheel with the hand already moving in the direction that the wheel is moving. I can't believe that more people are not using the Scullers Entry. It will be interesting to see what kind of flak I get at Craftsbury this year.

I like the analogy of cross country skiing, but the more I think about it, I'm afraid it's not quite as good as skate skiing. The advantage of skate skiing is that the skier is pushing off from the other foot, which is a moving platform. The skier keeps accelerating because he is accelerating from a platform that is moving at his present speed. The analogy would be perfect if we could somehow keep the oar blade moving toward the finish line while we pull on the oar handle. Unfortunately the oar blade is stuck in an almost fixed position in the water when we pull on the oar handle. I think the real advantage of the Scullers Entry is that it does not slow the system down like the typical entry with its backsplash, which is especially serious if we try to enter the

Endorsements

squared blade into the water as we approach the catch. The Scullers Entry does not slow the system, so in that sense it allows the system to accelerate. The system should accelerate as long as the water drag and our oar technique do less to slow the system down than pulling on the oar does to accelerate the system.

I really like the upside down bicycle experiment to describe the advantage of the Scullers Entry. I think the upside down bicycle experiment is what Vince is referring to on about page 38 of your book when he says "the wheel just turned faster and faster." If you get the wheel turning, squaring the blade and dropping it in at the catch is like grabbing the wheel and trying to rotate it faster. Squaring the blade and trying to enter it into the water as you approach the catch is like moving your hand opposite to the direction of rotation while you try to grab the wheel to then rotate it faster. Both approaches actually slow down the wheel before trying to rotate it faster. The Scullers Entry avoids slowing down the wheel and just tries to rotate it faster by contacting the wheel with the hand already moving in the direction of rotation, which is what people actually do when they try to accelerate the wheel.

- Steve Haase, Masters Sculler

The Quantum Sculler

Hi Jim,

I think you manage to capture the essence and appeal of single sculling and put it in a really good context. The references, quotes and analogies all support your view and reinforce the art of sculling and rowing. This reinforces the art in the sculler's implementation on the handles as well as in the coaching.

I would have a leg emphasis earlier in the stroke, but am happy to debate the merit or otherwise! I think it's very good and very important that you publish these views, Jim. They make us all reflect on our practices and how rowing fits into our and the athletes' lives.

When I was reading your paper, I was thinking about an area that I also think has some merit in the crew boats. It relates a bit to your nature awareness. Entrainment is a natural phenomenon, where animals and people can read and respond to each other's physiological signals. You can see it in flocks of birds and schools of fish where there is some form of instinctive communication that makes them move and behave as an entity en masse, coming closer together when threatened or navigating on a migration. When a group of women spend a lot of time together their monthly cycles fall into sync.

I don't have any hard research on this, but I suspect this entrainment happens in the crew boats to add to the psychological side you describe. This is where the crew is in total sync and there is plenty of work on the spoon, but they are in ultimate sync with each other and their physiology, which means higher speed at a lower physiological cost.

So there you go with a bit of my unorthodoxy! Well done again with the paper. Glad it's being published.

- Paul Thompson

Head Sculling Coach for Great Britain's National Team

Deeply impressed Jimmy, some of your best writing, integrating the subtle technical aspects with the overall flow of the stroke, a continuous cycle of change. This integration is your strength and uniqueness. What technical rowing coach could not be impressed? The Joy of Sculling Conference attendees should see this. Thank you.

- David Meggyesy, author of *Out of Their League*

Jimmy,

You must know how important your writing and the perspective you lay out is for many, many rowers. In fact many who don't even realize it, because what you write reflects the most comprehensive and truer understanding of the nature of Reality, and somewhere in their beings they resonate with it. We are in a time of a major paradigm shift, 'whole systems transition' as some have said. We are coming out of a 400 year major blind spot which says the universe is dead, consciousness is an artifact of brain chemistry and the only reality is the material one. How ass backwards can one get. On the contrary, the universe is alive and conscious, the brain translates and expresses Consciousness and behind the perceived material reality is Intelligence and Consciousness itself, which the great quantum physicists understood. Bringing rowing into alignment with this truer view of Reality is what you have done Jimmy. Bravo!

It is a pleasure to know you and appreciate the work you have done to lay this out for all of us. A huge thank you.

- David Meggyesy

Jimmy,

I very much enjoyed reading your wonderful essay. It is a very impressive culmination of all your previous writings. You have done great work in transferring Bohm's concept of "unbroken wholeness" in physics to the world of sculling and, indeed, all of life. I was struck by the number of important ideas in your essay that grow out of your concept of "wholeness" -- flow, cycle, integration, balance, connection, perception, understanding, consciousness and, ultimately, integrity and serenity. At its deepest level, your essay is a meditation on how we can be "at one" with our life, our undertakings, and the physical and spiritual world around us. I think this is what Jesus meant when He said, "the Kingdom of God is within you" (Luke 17:21). Jesus was telling us that the human and the Divine (the physical and the spiritual) are meant to be joined, not separated, and we should therefore live in a way that achieves wholeness and integrity with God's creation. Indeed, Tolstoy used Jesus' saying as the title for his great treatise on nonviolence, which had a profound influence on Gandhi and many others. As you point out, the modern world too often celebrates fragmentation, division, brute power, "winning at all costs" and "control" over others (rather than mastery over oneself). Another saying of Jesus is pertinent here: "first take the plank out of your own eye, and then you will see clearly to remove the speck from your brother's eye" (Matthew 7:5). Only if we achieve self-mastery through the disciplined pursuit of wholeness and integrity, as you describe so well, can we hope to offer meaningful advice and assistance to our brothers and sisters. [1]

Your additional section on the consciousness levels of beginning and intermediate scullers is a great addition to *The Quantum Sculler*. Your continued focus on wholeness, flow and swing will be of great help to new scullers and their teachers. I particularly liked your reference to "pulling what you can handle" during the drive, which is similar to your advice that the sculler can improve his or her technique more effectively by rowing at 90% effort rather than 100%.

Your idea of "pulling what you can handle" very much connects to my understanding of self-mastery. Your

---

[1] Correspondence from Art Wilmarth, former Yale oarsman and now Professor of Law at George Washington University, June 2014. Art has won a case in the Supreme Court of the United States.

idea carries interesting echoes from the Serenity Prayer (or, in a more abbreviated version, the precept of "let go and let God"), which to me conveys the same essential message. It is also interesting that the traditional concept of "master" included someone who had "mastered" his craft through long study and rigorous discipline and was then qualified to pass on his expertise to apprentices, who in turn would become masters themselves. The modern world seems to have lost sight of the concept of the master craftsman, in the same way that the modern legal profession emphasizes the role of adversarial "advocates" and no longer uses the wonderful term "Counsellor at Law" to describe the work of attorneys. (If you watch old reruns of "Perry Mason" from the 1950s, you will hear references to "Counsellor," but those references disappear from later shows and movies about lawyers.) How much better the legal profession would be today if lawyers still viewed their helping role as "counsellors" as being more important than their adversarial role as "advocates." You should be very proud of your status as a supreme "master craftsman" of sculling. I'm delighted that you are continuing to refine and convey the very important discoveries you've made about both sculling and life! [2]

- Art Wilmarth

former Yale Lightweight oarsman;

Professor of Law, George Washington University.

---

[2] Additional correspondence from Art Wilmarth, May 2014

Endorsements

Jimmy,

    This is a refreshing and inspiring book. At first it is easy to imagine that you have opened a passage in *The Prophet*, or, if you are old enough, you may have flashbacks to Sartre's existentialism. The clear message is to live in the present and to shed our tendency as scullers or coaches to fragment the process of moving the body, shell and blades with the water. A purist might question the analogy with the quantum model where energy is found in discrete packets or states but the message of interconnectedness in all things is still clearly expressed. Deceptively simplistic in approach, it contains a lifetime of observation and sensitive coaching. Anyone who teaches physical skills will benefit from reading this, particularly as it serves to remind us that our rational tendency to compartmentalize a chain into its individual links can often lead to confusion and frustration rather than the desired achievement of flow. Experience enables us to spot a problem in a link, but can blind us to the importance of remaining focused on the whole continuous process. This book draws attention to the need for a meditative awareness of ourselves, the tools, and the environment. Scullers will find clear instructions to smooth their skills both mentally and physically. To the uninitiated it may appear to assume knowledge of unfamiliar concepts but will inspire those who see the clues to explore further. For those of us who spend a lot of time alone on the water, it provides some excellent aids to visualization and awareness without the negative clutter of self-criticism, which can so often cause us to miss the pure pleasure of where we are and what a privilege it is to be there.

- Giuseppe Lund, Master Sculptor and Sculler

Jimmy,

I can only ask that you continue to write while in a flow state. It brings out the best of your coaching wisdom. I feel like we are on an adventure into uncharted territory, and Vince is right when he says we will be hit with some fairly colorful names, but the fact that we are coming together as a group gives us a little more heft as we take on the conventional coaching communities. Conventional, mechanistic coaching is not a bad thing; it just cannot teach athletes how to get into a flow state. For that, we need more holistic approaches such as those we are developing. I'm just glad to have found some holistic thinkers who are willing to investigate this new paradigm with me.

Anyway, I love what you have written. Vince Reynolds and I grew up playing sports the same way you did. Get the neighborhood kids together and go to the playground and play ball, go to the courts and play tennis, go to the field and play football. We didn't have any coaches, no instruction, just balls, bats, gloves, rackets and a deep desire to get better at what we were doing.

It was fun back then! What the hell happened?

- Scott Ford,
  Master Tennis Coach,
  author of *Welcome to the Zone: Peak Performance Redefined*

Table of Contents

Endorsements i
Introduction - David Meggyesy 1
Chapter One - A Sculler's Philosophy 6
Chapter Two - Specific Movement Phases 27
Chapter Three - Integrated Drive and Release 40
Chapter Four – Active Recovery and Sculler's Entry 55
Chapter Five - Trunk Swing 85
Chapter Six – The Simulation Exercises 93
Chapter Seven - Beyond Materialism 100
Chapter Eight - Training the Spirit 113
Chapter Nine - The Imaginative Mind 146
Chapter Ten - Complexity and Consciousness 152
Chapter Eleven - Conservation 174
Chapter Twelve - Simplicity 194
Chapter Thirteen - Slow Motion Movement 196
Chapter Fourteen - Continuous Body Movement 204
Chapter Fifteen - Level Run of the Shell 209
Chapter Sixteen - The Flow State 214
Chapter Seventeen - Sculling as an Art Form 233
Chapter Eighteen - Summary 245
Afterword 260
Appendix - Movement Training Drills 263
Bibliography 271
Acknowledgements 273
About the Author 275

The Quantum Sculler

Introduction

It's a great art, is rowing. It's the finest art there is. It's a symphony of motion. And when you're rowing well, why it's nearing perfection. And when you near perfection, you're touching the Divine. It touches the you of you. Which is your soul.
- George Yeoman Pocock

The Love of Doing It
- Lao Tzu

Master Coaches have known and taught that the essence of sport is spiritual development. Spiritual development means the development, integration and expression of body, mind, soul and spirit and all the various aspects of our human experience, which culminates in a profound feeling, flowing, knowing sense of Interconnection, Unity and Oneness with all existence. It is about Waking Up. In modern parlance, we call it dropping into the Zone or the Flow State. This state is a verb, not a noun, an ever-changing process of revelation. As athletes, when we experience and integrate these dimensions of our being, when our symphony is playing well, we enter Flow as we engage in our sport and we touch the Divine.

Jim Joy is a Master Rowing Coach in a lineage of Master Rowing Coaches including his mentor, Robert Fitzpatrick. Master Coaches also know that their teaching is about unleashing and integrating the enormous power and presence that we all really are. Expressing this sensibility and awareness through our sport and in our lives. When it happens in rowing, we drop into Flow, where no boundaries or separation exist between ourselves, the shell, the oars, the water and the world surrounding us. We become whole and one with. And for the practical and measurement minded, excellent performance is typically the result.

Master Coaches emphasize focus on Excellence and Mastery and being in the present, not on winning or losing. They know that with fully engaged focus on the Present Moment and Excellence, winning and losing will take care of themselves. "The goal was always to row our best possible race on the day," said budding Master Coach and Olympian, Jason Dorland, regarding his high school crew who were competing in England's 2014 Henley Royal Regatta.

Contemporary coaching is undergoing a significant transformation with the incorporation of mindset or inner game training. Jim Joy is a pioneer in this regard and the coaching world is starting to catch up. The old saw that athletic performance is

The Quantum Sculler

90% mental is being taken seriously by coaches who are learning to use inner game perspectives and practices to improve their coaching and their athletes' performance. Typically, coaches pay lip service to the importance of the mental part of the game, yet don't know how to teach or incorporate inner game training into their overall training program. Telling an athlete to focus and not teaching the athlete how to focus is basically useless. It is like telling an athlete to be strong and not showing them how to strength train.

Many of these useful consciousness perspectives and technologies have come from the world's spiritual traditions, quantum physics, energy psychology, sports psychology, and the human potential movement. They focus on athletes turning their attention inward to an awareness of their thought processes, their emotions and body energy states. Various techniques to quiet and focus the mind, meditation and mindfulness training and dealing with dysfunctional emotional states via Emotional Freedom Technique (EFT), and body energy scanning are some examples of practices coaches are beginning to use.

Through Jim's 23 years of leading his Joy of Sculling Conferences and in two previous books, *The Minds Eye* and *Hanlan's Spirit*, inner awareness perspectives and practices have been presented to the rowing coaching community. In addition, Jim's work with college crews and his individual coaching with

Introduction

emerging masters sculling champion, Vince Reynolds, and other top-flight scullers, has produced remarkable results.

In my view, Jim's major contribution is his integral approach to coaching rowing. It is a holistic perspective, emphasizing the whole stroke cycle versus emphasis on the component parts. In this view, the whole stroke cycle is primary (the whole is bigger than the sum of its parts) and supersedes the component parts of the stroke, versus the parts being primary to the whole. In other words, the elements of the stroke, blade entry for example, is taught as a flowing integrated component connected with all the other dimensions of the stroke cycle. The aim is to achieve a seamless whole stroke cycle. In addition, Jim emphasizes an integrated "feel" of the cycle, where the stroke components are naturally felt flowing into each other. And each stroke cycle is unique. Not only is Jim a master of integration, he is a master of the details of the component parts of the stroke cycle.

The combination of technical proficiency and Jim's holistic approach is the stepping-stone to fully experience the cyclic flow of rowing and a deeper feeling, a joyful sense of integration and unity with boat, water and environment. In this way, through rowing and by extension all sport; our larger nature, some would say, "our super nature that presses to be born in us", is revealed. In fact, sport is routinely revealing our "supernatures", our vast human potential. It seems, not a day goes by

The Quantum Sculler

when an athlete has not broken a previous world record. The emergence of new sports, skate and snow boarding for example, and "extreme" acrobatic sports is truly breathtaking.

There is deeper promise offered by sport. Our powerful unique human activity can reveal our vast potentials, our larger nature, and profound realization of our identity with all there is. *The Quantum Sculler* is a bell weather book, pointing the way via sport to our larger, deeper life, for which, we all know and yearn.

- David Meggyesy, 15 January 2015

Chapter One - A Sculler's Philosophy

A Sculler's Philosophy

The process involves our love of the Earth and the Universe beyond. Excellent guides are found in Heraclitus, Thomas Berry, Wendell Berry, Pierre Teilhard de Chardin, Brian Swinne, David Bohm, Meister Eckhart, and the old sculler and master builder, George Pocock.

Guidance is sought from our ponds, rivers, lakes, and even our oceans. We seek to engage the Earth on our hikes to the countryside woods and to the nearby glens and ravines. We embrace the Natural World.

Our spirit is renewed and the plasticity of our minds permits us to include wholeness and integration. St. Francis reminds us of the benefits from simplicity, economy, and gentle sharing as well as the experience of solitude, stillness, and silence.

All of this is woven into the fabric of the sculling stroke.

- Jimmy Joy

David Bohm expressed his concern over the fragmented state of our minds and the world at large, "For fragmentation is now very widespread, not only throughout society, but also in each individual; and this is leading to a kind of general confusion of the mind, which creates an endless series of problems and interferes with our clarity of perception, so seriously as to prevent us from being able to solve most of them... The notion that all of these fragments are separately existent is evidently an illusion, and this illusion cannot do other than lead to endless conflict and confusion." [3]

Our commitment to preserve and develop a human quality of life involves the common responsibility of us all. To complete this objective we must be connected with each other and for the sculler, similarly, the reality of the cyclical stroke, it is one piece without fragmentation. It is a beautiful whole movement that enhances the quality of life for the sculler. The athlete must be aware that smooth muscle action, the fluid, continuous transitions at the release and the entry, the timing and precision involved in the recovery and the drive phases, and the overall consistent rhythm and flow in the stroke cycle, along with the raw strength involved in each pull of the oar, are the factors that make the shell run exceedingly well. These are the qualities that cannot be obtained from the statistical charts. These important qualities must be observed and evaluated by the coach.

For the sculler, a strong bond exists between his body, the shell, and the water; the flow state permeates this integrated

---

[3] David Bohm, *Wholeness and the Implicate Order*, p.1.

stroke. In addition, the Sculler's being sees life as an interconnection between things and humans. There is no separation as he views the natural world. This is not the usual picture that most people have of the world. It is exceptional but it is a state of mind that is beneficial for the accomplished sculler to develop. With this state of mind he approaches the Divine.

Each morning upon rising from night's slumber, I begin the day by thinking of whole, in my thoughts, in my movements, and my perception of the world around me, especially when I look at our back gardens. The athlete developing this perspective can easily see the connection between himself, his equipment, and the water. All the externals have a life, from which he can find personal identification. His life and sculling can become deeply ecological.

This is an evolutionary process; much like his life as a person; the coach and the athlete are evolving in their consciousness and skill level. Sculling is not just being, it is becoming. The athlete evolves over the course of a training period, a few months, a year. Both the small movements and the larger parts of the stroke undergo a metamorphosis. Nothing is static in life and the athlete's skill and consciousness are highly transformational. They are unfinished and must be surpassed or completed. We have to lay out the process needed for this completion. The consciousness requires the daily dosage of meditation with the deep, whole body breathing. Skill training requires the daily prescription of the appropriate drilling on the parts. It is a mental and physical evolutionary process. It is a deep study in which the coach and athlete are involved. It spills over into their everyday lives. You cannot escape it. It requires a deep education and a serious commitment to this holistic course of action.

We must investigate every aspect of our training and be conscious of the parallel situations in our lives. We must realize that we are completely malleable. We are capable of great changes in our mental and physical and technical frameworks. Modern science recognizes the plasticity of our mental and physical being; in particular, we can't remain static in our thinking when facing the numerous possibilities of making technical and mental improvements. Over a season we can see the body become more refined, similarly, we must witness the same evolution with our consciousness. The athlete simply becomes more knowledgeable and his awareness increases. The athlete becomes more selective in how he moves and flows more subtlety over the slide bed. From the complexity and integration of the movements involved, an evolution of a progressively more conscious mind evolves.

Technically, there are three places in the stroke cycle that lead to a pause or hesitation in the movements.

- One, is the early rollup of the blade to the squared position above the water causing a definite pause in the movement of the blade.
- Two, is the severe break in the inside wrist at the release and the use of heavy energy to release and feather the blade by this single wrist action, rather than using a two handed roll release with minimal wrist action.
- Three, is the principle of holding on with the arms during the early stages of the drive; this use of the arms works in combination with the fragmented legs and trunk action.

All three actions are based on a static idea of movement rather than a dynamic principle. These three rough actions do not fit with the world of wholeness, connections, and smooth movement. None of these actions will lead to the optimal Flow State. In contrast, the sculler's entry does lead to Flow. "Moreover, it's not just a world *out there* that is moving; it's also a world *in here*." [4] We are highly malleable and can experience and develop the plasticity of the body and mind.

The cycle is a constantly changing, pulsating, rhythmic, and continuous motion. These pauses in the action are definitely

---

[4] Carter Phipps, *Evolutionaries*, p.28

out of synch with the larger quantum world in which we live. It is a world of constant movement. All three pauses can be eliminated through proper quantum sculling measures: the two movement entry action in place of the conventional three phase motion, the fingers release with minimal wrist action, and, the whole body drive, with no fragmentation.

It is quite a different coaching perspective when you accept the world of constant change. For the Quantum coach, the stroke cycle has one slight pause of the seat at the release with the arms continuing the movement with the two handed release (sweep rowing) and follow through.

This book explores the world of wholeness in its approach to the training of the various movements. We feel that to fragment the various movements is not an effective way to move up and down the slide. The recognition and adoption of wholeness in our stroke and our lives parallels the way the quantum world works. This worldview relies heavily on relationships and connections recognizing that everything is connected. The coaching utilizes cooperation and substantive relationships. In some ways the training is a reactionary method in that we rely partially on the experiences of the early professional scullers. It was these professional scullers, who were competing for large sums, yet held an operating standard in their sculling that was head and shoulders above the amateurs of their day. These workingmen seriously studied their shells, the various effects of water conditions, and the training of their bodies. They were the first professional students of the sport.

In exploring wholeness we must consider all the various sciences, physics, biology, mechanics, neuroscience, as well as the important dimension of movement training, the periodization of training, the psychology, the meditative practices, philosophy, nutrition, and the critical yogic and flexibility practices. So it is an *integral* approach to training that is embraced by the coach and the athlete. It is a life practice encompassing activity in and out of the shell. So they, the coach and the athlete, are constantly looking for new ways and information on preparing, staging and executing the training. Possibly, the one glaring shortcoming of the present day training methods is the scarce attention given to understanding the movements and the training of these critical movements. The other pronounced shortcoming is the serious lack of consideration for the development of the inner athlete.

There can be a deeper and more meaningful value for sport and the rowing practice in the 21st century. The goal in training the athlete is to have him or her experience the highest levels of consciousness and skill. To facilitate this development, we, the coach, as well as the athlete, must embrace the idea of wholeness in training the athlete's body and mind. Such a pursuit engages our total being; spiritually, mentally, and bodily. This pursuit demands a high degree of concentrated intensity in our practice sessions. It requires being very aware and attentive. It is a dance in the shell that the athlete is performing. Each dimension of this routine must be honed and refined. We must do this even during the work pieces. As an example, we cannot be so concentrated on the numbers on the ergometer that we forego the precision required to execute the movements effectively. Don't overlook the technical component when you apply the work.

This type of thinking, and the use of the body, covers all of our activity. We must abandon our phones and iPads. It is a path well beyond the preoccupation with winning. We, coach and athlete, must operate totally in the moment. We must concentrate and give careful attention to our posture, our alignment, and the movement patterns of our sport. We are trying to reach the correct levels of movement to optimize our strength. In rowing, we are encouraged to pull what we can handle. There is no grimacing of the facial features, no over exertion of the limb actions, and no straining. Consequently, there is a sustained flowing action to the movement of the whole body. It is simultaneously powerful and graceful. It is an art form.

I am reminded of a story by the late Frank Cunningham (*The Sculler at Ease*). He immediately goes back to the day when he was an undergraduate at Harvard University and his coach at the time was the incomparable Bert Haines, "Myself and a teammate were out in singles and we met with Bert out on the water, Cunningham recalled. He was in his single and when we had our bows on his stern, we didn't say anything, but we just looked at each other and started pushing. We pushed for about 10 minutes and then we looked around and he was still there. So we pushed a little harder until finally, we just gave up. He was just playing with us. He wasn't laughing, but he was amused. And a few things came to mind. I realized I was in the presence of one of the finest scullers I had ever met and that I was watching a man that was three times my age doing something that I couldn't do. I was quietly impressed by that. The lesson for Cunningham on that day was that just pulling hard on a set of oars won't make a boat go fast. Good rowing takes skill and requires a feel for how a boat moves in the water." Frank Cunningham would go on and teach the sculling skills to countless people for the remainder of his life. He learned the lessons well from his English mentor Bert Haines.

By concentrating solely on the score or the number, the athlete loses touch with the skill and the artistry. The physicist Bohm felt that reality could not be described statistically and that reality lends itself much more to the way of understanding one might have of the arts, of poetry, pottery, and dance. The coach has to provide the philosophical leadership. He has to be the supreme artist and conductor. He has to maintain a view of the whole movement and not get distracted by a fragmented approach to the skill learning. He must weave the athlete and his shell into the whole surrounding environment. With the right perceptions of things we experience a living cosmology.

Personal mental strength is always considered the ability to focus for long periods of time on a chosen topic, at the exclusion of everything else that is going on around you. This is a quality that is so required during the long winter months in the eastern part of the country, when the athlete is doing his daily simulation exercises. He must develop this ability to concentrate, and his ability to be attentive for long periods. By doing so he enters the mysterious dimension of the artist.

Simon Verity, reflecting on his passion for stone cutting, said this, "I've had moments of real connection with my work. I feel it as if a spark has leapt and then it's gone. These moments are not continuous. I keep trying to get more of a flow, to allow more without trying to control so much. How can we extend these moments of connection? That's the question, and that is what is so painful. You must have this sense of this opening, this other energy passing through, and it's utter bliss when it happens, but it is transitory. I think that this is what any artist is searching for. What drives you on is that it's there and it's just a question of getting out of the way." This is the approach the athlete must have, when he is doing the simulation exercises indoors on the rowing ergometer. He must be open to develop a strong sense of visualizing the stroke.

A Sculler's Philosophy

In a similar fashion, the coach removes the unnecessary movements in the athlete's stroke cycle as he works to improve the athleticism. He is doing the work of a sculptor.

Tracy Cochran, writing about the work of Simon Verity, observed, "Very slowly over many years, I learned that consenting to be with what is, body, heart, and mind, without judging or seeking to change anything, in any way, allows a new energy or vibration or feeling of life to appear - and this is the truth I was searching for. The truth can be found only in the moment. One moment we are fully embodied beings, sensing and feeling the world around us and inside us, opening to perceptions of reality that lead us towards a living unknown. As a stone carver, Simon Verity told me, a connection with the infinite can appear in the midst of attending to something very finite." [5]

This situation of integration occurs to us as we address the repetitive nature of the stroke cycle. We can feel the connection first with our immediate environment, the shell and the water, and then to the larger world around us. It has this quality of being in touch with the infinite. Remember, we are doing the great work of the artist when we learn to scull. We are touching the infinite.

The quantum physicist, David Bohm, states that we can look at reality as having two levels. He refers to the level we inhabit

---

[5] *Seeking Verity,* by Tracy Cochran, Parabola Winter 2013-4 /13

The Quantum Sculler

where toaster ovens and humans appear to be separate from one another. This is what he termed The Explicate Order. The level of reality where quantum interconnectedness reigns, and all things become a seamless and unbroken whole, he calls this The Implicate Order.[6] With an awareness of the principles of this new physics, the coach and sculler can come to recognize this sub atomic reality, where everything is a whole and interconnected. The consciousness of the sculler must attempt to be totally aware and concentrating on feeling this Implicate Order. We can feel this when we sit in meditation to the degree that we feel the various parts of our body tingling, itching, pulsing, or throbbing.[7] This is an excellent example of engaging the whole of the body. We can also feel it in our slow motion sculling when we feel the deeper connections involved with performing the stroke. Our awareness level must attempt to feel the energy bands that surround our bodies. We begin to feel this sheath of energy that envelops our bodies in our daily meditative sitting. We can attempt to feel the energy from the water when we are in the shell through our sculls. The oar placement at blade depth distinguishes this sensation. What we can do in sculling is attempt to mirror the reality of the interconnectedness of the sub atomic level through our concentration and

---

[6] Michael Talbot, *Mysticism and the New Physics*, p.158.
[7] Will Johnson, *Yoga and the Mahamudra*, p. 91

A Sculler's Philosophy

meditative practices. Thus, we come to view the stroke cycle with all of its parts as an integrated whole. So the Implicate Order can be viewed as the foundation of Flow. If we can relate our minds to the Implicate Order, we can begin to achieve Flow. This is what expert tennis coach and writer Scott Ford identifies as the "parallel mode of operation." It is correlated with an interior state of integrated consciousness.[8] In the integral system the whole is primary in stark contrast to the mechanistic system's view that sees the parts as primary to the whole. It is nonlinear and rational rather than mechanistic.

To further our connection to the Implicate level, we have to be whole and connect with the world around us. At the boathouse on the canal, it means taking a few moments to look around you and see how you connect to the trees, to water, to the birds in flight, to the deer, and to the beavers. See how we interact with the equipment, the dock, the coach, and with our teammates. Everything is all part of this magnificent dance of life and sculling. There is a flow to this whole scene, "this tapestry," that must encompass us. We have to attempt to feel it. So we have to become more aware and conscious of the activity that is taking place in our immediate surroundings, right in front of our eyes.

---

[8] Scott Ford, *Quadratic Relativity Fields: Modeling Human Performance*, p. 7.

The Quantum Sculler

"Do you realize, sir, that you are the world and the world is you? The world is not separate from you and me. There is a common thread of relationship weaving us all together. Deep down, we are all totally connected. Superficially, things appear separate. Separate species, separate races, separate cultures and colors, separate nationalities and religions and politics. If you look closely, you will immediately see that we all part of a great tapestry of life." [9] This is a passage from the work of Satish Kumar that parallels the social implications of Bohm's Quantum Physics. We are all part of a greater whole. David Bohm was extremely insightful as he projected his physics findings to the larger world around him.

We can relate to these writings when we engage in the continuity of the sculling stroke. The complete picture of the sculler is that there is no break in the whole movement. The relaxed fingers, hands and arms are connected to the trunk swing that is carried by the firm application of the legs. All of this is accomplished with the perfected sliding of the shell through the water.

"For example, because we are constituted out of this non-local level, Bohm feels it is ultimately meaningless to speak of consciousness as having a specific location. It may manifest in our heads while we function in life, but the true home of con-

---

[9] Satish Kumar, *You Are, Therefore I Am*, p.91

sciousness is in The Implicate says Bohm. Thus, consciousness, the great ocean of consciousness that has divided itself up into all human beings, also exists in all things." [10]

Coaching sculling reflects Bohm's Implicate Order. Each segment of the stroke cycle is treated as a whole - the release, the recovery, the entry, and the drive. The drills for each part should also be treated as a whole in the minds of the athlete and the coach. So, when you drill at quarter slide, you actually are going through the whole of the stroke cycle. The cycle becomes actually, two complete parts of the whole, the entry and drive, and the release and recovery. With this teaching approach there is a significantly reduced emphasis on the parts and the whole becomes more prominent. There is a significant adjustment in the consciousness of the sculler and for the coach. However, it is a perfect lead in to flow. You never stray far from the wholeness of the cycle. It involves a different vision; a different mental perception; and a different set of eyes. Awareness takes over from instinct. Awareness is our attention to the whole of life. We come to realize how much we live our lives in fragments. It is the awareness of how we speak; what we say; how we walk, what we think. [11] We engage more in feeling, than in thought.

---

[10] Michael Talbot, *Mysticism and the New Physics*, p.158.
[11] J. Krishnamurti, *Freedom from the Known*, p.33.

The Quantum Sculler

A friend, David Meggyesy, a former NFL player and now a recreational sculler, has this reaction to the process learning to scull, "Reality is cyclical change. I was again aware of that fact this morning, with spring booming here. My thought was the stroke cycle is a cycle reflecting all the cycles within cycles that are the process of constant change or flux, manifesting reality and evolution, the Buddha and others have noted. How we actualize or become aware of these various cycles of change, and they have their own characteristics in all that we do and, certainly in how we cycle and flow with the boat and water in the stroke – is what you are teaching, Jimmy – yes?" [12]

In classical, Newtonian physics there is little regard for this integrative perspective that everything is moving. In sculling it is the sculler, the shell, and the water. Yet, everything is vibrating. There is no preparation of the blade, no setting of the trunk angle. The blade and trunk actions must be a moment in the present. Otherwise, it becomes a moment in the past. The mind, in thinking preparation, is in the wrong place. It is in the future, rather than being in the present.

When I sit each morning in meditation, I find the rug undulating, like a wave and a particle. So nothing is fixed and we must keep this in mind as we perform the stroke cycle. We must remain in the present throughout this cycle.

---

[12] Correspondence from David Meggyesy, May 2, 2014.

A Sculler's Philosophy

Scott Ford reminds us that "The human peak performance state is definitely *not* about playing in the past. One of the primary characteristics of flow, reported by athletes from around the world, is the sense of being 'in the present.' Anyone who has ever been in the zone, knows the feeling of total presence, the sense of being one with the game, one with the flow of the action, right here, right now." [13]

David Bohm makes it clear when he writes, "In this flow, mind and matter are not separate substances. Rather, they are different aspects of one whole and unbroken movement." [14]

For all of this detail, you simply move between the two major points of the release and the entry in continuous motion, with a highly compact, consistent, and standard movement. It is highly contained, because there are no extraneous movements. It is pure economy. The rhythm of the movement parallels the reality of our world. It resonates. It flows. Thus our consciousness is integrated. It is refined from the earlier rough stages of development.

The flow of the movement was something that I discovered one evening, long ago in St. Catharines on the Henley course. I never forgot that experience. It still remains vivid in my memory bank. It was such an exhilarating discovery, the

---

[13] Scott Ford, *Quadratic Relativity Fields: Modeling Human Performance*, p.5
[14] David Bohm, *Wholeness and the Implicate Order*, p. 14.

complete connection between me and the shell. The shell simply slid through the water so effortlessly. This occurred during my second year of sculling. My body swing was married to the flowing movement of the shell. It was a magnificent feeling of lightness and ease.

Everything about the stroke was connected, whole, and continuous; the entry to the drive, to the release and follow through, to the easy movements of the recovery. It was an exhilarating feeling. The simple flow between the release and the entry became consistent and repetitive. This is where my consciousness expanded to include me, the shell, and the water. All these ingredients have a life that came together. It is quality that has to become the normal operating procedure, rather than the random. For me it happened, and is still there today, each time that I venture into a shell. I can feel the shell respond immediately to my blade entry, and I can feel the pronounced swing from the hips. So it becomes, not only a physical action, but a state of mind.

Vince Reynolds, a masters sculler, wrote recently, "this paper with all your thoughts is brilliant, elegant, flows and speaks of who you are and what you speak. It is beautiful. You can feel the power and the energy that flows forth from the simplicity and the movement within the words. I think that is because it is what quantum sculling is about." [15]

There are many parts to be mastered -- the entry, the release, the recovery, the drive, as well as the practice of the pulling what you can handle, the high rate clean sprints, the slow motion, the 90% law, and the mind pieces. But, all these parts and practices, must, at some point, come together in a unified whole. It is the attention to the details of the movement that leads the sculler invariably to the flow state and to a life of making connections in his life out of the shell.

With relaxation comes an elongated spine and a hollow tube for a body, where our cellular energy can flow. There is the stark difference between the solid bamboo and the hollow bamboo. The solid bamboo has thick walls and a narrow opening, whereas the hollow bamboo has thin walls and a large central opening. It is the hollow bamboo that facilitates movement of energy in the body. [16]

All of this creates the elusive Flow in the whole of the system. It becomes a study of effortlessness. The work is there, but the sculler doesn't appear to be working. This unified whole distinguishes the uniqueness of the sculler. There is a built-in relief to the physiology with this type of continuous movement. In-

---

[15] Correspondence from Vince Reynolds
[16] Will Johnson, *Yoga of the Mahamudra*, p. 64

ternally, the sculler's body is simply operating more efficiently. There is no beginning and no end to the movement. It is simply a dance, a movement that continues intuitively and endlessly.

At some point the movement becomes part of a much deeper spiritual side to the participant. We begin to relate this subtle movement to the whole of our life beyond the shell. Thus, it is a quality that the sculler carries over into his life. It is the work ethic, the conservation, the subtleness, and the continuity of movement, that expresses itself in everything that the athlete does. He observes how his mind functions. There is little separation between himself as a person and himself as an athlete. He is constantly aware of his movements, no matter where he is. His various lives and life experience become one. He is the same constant person.

All of this is part of his spirituality. In turn, the coach has a heightened awareness of flow and how it encapsulates every aspect of his own life. He constantly monitors both his physical movements through proprioception and the movements of his thoughts through attention. It is a significant attempt on his part to live his life as an example of Flow. It is in the little things of life that this can occur, like washing the dinner dishes, as well as the larger situations that face us.

We must become careful in the use of measuring in our sculling practice, because it might become more gross and mechanical. There is far too much measurement going on. We forget that we have to concentrate on the details of improving the mechanics. This is especially true with Flow; it is a reality that is immeasurable.

With Flow and identifying with the Implicate, the sculler feels that he is part of a greater whole as he looks around himself. The people in the street, in the supermarket, his neighbors and beyond his borders are all part of his empathetic system. He feels deeply, and all this feeling derives from the simple, whole, continuous movement in a fragile shell. The parts and the whole are graceful, smoothly elegant, and almost artful.

Chapter Two - Specific Movement Phases

Teaching movements, not style, not technique. Narrowing, enlarging the focus and separating the process into two large motions: the Drive and Release, follow through; secondly, the Recovery and Entry, the Sculler's Entry! Revolutionary, maybe, but certainly thoughtful! There are two wholes, with our methodology paralleling the Quantum world. The details emerge later in the process. We are pruning. Simplicity is our goal. We are reducing the words. We are operating close to Flow, to Bohm's Implicate Level and definitely in the Intuitive Mode. The Novice Sculler can handle it!

- Jimmy Joy

Have the young athlete sit at the release position and then provide detailed instruction on how to hold the handle. This is the initial order of teaching for any and all of the "implement" sports such as tennis, baseball, golf, hockey, lacrosse and of course, sculling. When the blade is squared in the water, the handhold should be a "monkey grip" with the fingers, and with the palms off the handle surface. The third knuckle line should be on top of the mid-handle and the wrists must be flat. In

Specific Movement Phases

sweep rowing, it is a finger hold with the inside thumb lightly touching the handle during the drive and recovery phases. There is no squeezing of the handle by the thumbs. With this minimal action by the thumb, the release does not become a function of the wrist action. The release is completed with the absolute minimum of noise. The words from the coach should be kept to a minimum. Let the young novice explore and allow him time to get the feel for the handles.

    The instruction for the actual movements is divided into two wholes, first, the drive through to the release and second, the recovery phase culminating in the entry. So we begin with the Integrated Drive from the entry position to the release movements. This is an easy way for the novice to begin his start in sculling, because, with the blades in the water, his balance is established. Immediately, the novice gets a feel for the balance. You emphasize that the blade moves through the water at blade depth. With this, he also gets a feel for where his hands should be in space. He is encouraged to pull with his hands close together. He is positioned at the entry (his definition of where he is comfortable, 1/4 to 3/4 slide) with the blade at blade depth. Then he focuses on the even pull, feeling the constant pressure on the blade face as it moves through the water. So he begins the process of concentrating. His sense of feel should become heightened as he draws the blade through the water. Good posture is emphasized as well as the whole body involvement. He releases the blade and follows through with his arm action from the elbows (the anconeous muscles). He pauses with the body slightly through the perpendicular and the knees up a little. If he is not comfortable with this exercise, have him sit at the release position and have him do some light sculling with the arms only. It is important for the novice to know immediately that the two hands work closely together, one above the other. You don't want a large gap between the two hands at any point in the stroke cycle. A large space between the hands creates an imbalance. Perception is important at this point in the single. It is the perception of where the hands are in space. Make sure that the two hands are level at the release of the blade from the water.

Then come the movements of the recovery and the entry that are the second half of the two-part instruction package. The hand position must be addressed continually in the early stages of instruction. The finger engagement is stressed, as well as the relationship of the handhold to the overall movements. The hold of the handle is an integral part of these movements.

In sculling, the thumbs are positioned over the ends of the grips. Through the thumbs, lateral pressure is exerted on the sculls and this helps with the balance of the shell. On the ergometer, stress a narrower hold with the thumbs positioned at the point on the handle, where it angles upward toward the chain. So the hands are separated by about eight inches. This will help to keep the stroke more streamlined. It is also advised that the athletes row the erg with their shoes off so that they can feel the movements more with their feet.

Along with this posture of the hands on the handle, the sitting posture is addressed. The carriage must be upright and relaxed, combined with even pressure on each buttocks. The lower back remains straight throughout the whole movement. Any reaching with the trunk is from the hips. The lower back remains straight. So, it is critical that the athlete be flexible in the hip region of his body.

At this point, it is advisable to have the sculler sit at the release position with the forearms angled from the trunk and in the line of pull. The shoulders should be down, with the hand height equal to the length of the upper arms. There is no hunching of the shoulders. Everything is relaxed. The trunk is positioned at approximately 15 degrees beyond the perpendicular. With this position the sculler can now come directly forward out of bow, moving directly towards the entry.

This is the point at which I began my sculling instructions, and subsequently, it was the same point that I began to teach sculling. We stayed at this point until the movement had been mastered. This was the hallmark of Robert Fitzpatrick's teaching -- mastering each of the movements, eliminating any extraneous motions. He was committed to producing an athlete in the shell. He was committed to the making of the sculler. So many people, who are sluggers, claimed to be sculling. This important distinction was clear in his mind and in his teaching - are you a sculler or a slugger?

The development of the oarsman must be viewed as the development of the complete athlete. The athlete operates from a sound posture at all points in the stroke cycle; he has to be centered over the narrow keel line. His position must also be well balanced as he moves quietly up and down the slide bed. He operates in a state of stillness during the drive, as he must be completely relaxed. Every aspect of his body, his hands, his arms, his legs, and his trunk should demonstrate this quality of relaxation. Relaxation allows for expression of power, reduces anxiety levels, and produces stillness in the body. Power comes from this stillness. It also produces the calm state of mind that is so essential for racing at your optimal level. When you are relaxed in the body and the mind, the energy will flow. In this state you are calm, relaxed, centered, grounded in your shell, and performing as a whole being.

Eventually, he must view himself as a dancer, an athlete; and above all as an artist. As an artist, he must seek and hold the smoothness of his movements. His body sketches perfection as he moves to and fro in the tiny shell. He operates and works his body with the shell as a state of wholeness between these two essential elements. But, in seeking and experiencing this ideal, the coach and the athlete utilize a huge range of lead-up activities including yoga, rope jumping, abdominal breathing techniques, meditation, movement training, simulation exercises, controlled strength and power exercises, running, balance exercises, both in and out of the shell, and focus and concentration drills. This holistic approach and practice becomes part of a very deep educational process for both the athlete and the coach. In each of these activities, the athlete must be aware of his posture, the degree of relaxation in his body movements, his balance, his alignment, the wholeness and the amount of stillness in the body. Every movement of the body seeks an ideal state of refinement and effortless power. With this approach the body takes on a quality of lightness in its movements; it is effortless. There has to be lightness to our step, to our gait, and to our striding with the shell. The easy striding and continuous sliding results from this continuous smooth muscle action. This quality originates with "the pulling what you can handle approach" on the drive, letting the shell run underneath you as you sit lightly on the seat during the recovery phase. These qualities go a long way toward establishing rhythm and flow in the stroke cycle. All of this is overlaid with a relaxed state of mind and body.

Here is a description of the wonderful German educator Rudolf Steiner, in the early years of the 20th Century, as he was observed walking to the podium:

> "Here was levity personified: the human body as rhythm assuming form. What impressed me so about this human

figure was the force of uprightness that supported his whole body. His head remained steady as he crossed the auditorium with a spring in his step. His light, rhythmic movements left me with the impression that the earth itself was connected to the rhythm of his walking. His posture was very erect yet fluid, his hands agile, and the movements of his head, which was held back a bit, yet tilted forward, were very rapid. Only an eagle stands like this." [17]

This is a much different state of mind from the current, conventional coaching approach of all-out 100% effort. The lightness and rhythmic movements of Rudolf Steiner are certainly qualities to strive for in our athletes. This process represents the twin development of consciousness and skill being accomplished. The skill in the hands really displays the evidence of this development. The hand movements at each end of the slide must be quick, relaxed, and agile. At every practice, there must be inserted into the program an opportunity to practice skillful hand actions. This is where slow motion rowing is so helpful. Stationary drills at the release and the entry allow the sculler to get a real feel for quickness and agility of the hands and fingers. As a young sculler, I learned so much watching coach Fitzpat-

---

[17] A description of the great German educator of the early 20th Century, Rudolf Steiner from *Rudolf Steiner as a Spiritual Teacher*.

rick's hands as he described the stroke mechanics. His simulations had a profound effect, something that I have never forgotten. I can still visualize him before me. He was more than a coach; he was an artist.

Movement training, with its daily round of drills, allows the athlete to effectively use all the other training practices. It maximizes the impact of strength, endurance, tolerance work, and quickness training undergone by the athlete. Even as you perform these part stroke drills, you are thinking whole stroke. The objective of the movement training is to develop smoothness and control. This might be said to be the primary purpose of all training. It unites all the ingredients in our training plan. It is this smooth, controlled movement that leads the athlete to the state of Flow. This is a refined state of movement, highly complex, yet simple in the delivery of the movement. It produces a highly developed consciousness in the athlete. This Flow experience involves the fluid, quick transitions at each end of the slide and the subtle coordinative movements in between these transitions. Thus, you must drill over and over on the parts viewed as segments of the whole. It was the wise Greek, Heraclitus, many years ago, who declared that, "everything is flux; nothing is stationary." So it is with the stroke cycle, all the parts are in motion. There is no setting of the trunk angle early in the recovery or squaring the blade above the water in preparation for the entry. The stroke cycle mirrors our lives and the quantum. We are continually experiencing change. Drilling makes the connections between the parts more subtle. This subtlety is connected to the ethic and practice of "pulling what you can handle." Then you are pulling and sculling with more sensitivity and smarter. You have this mind set with lifting of weights, your hill runs, your erg workouts, every training vehicle embraces this philosophy of work.

There are no details offered to the athlete at this point. He is encouraged from the beginning to explore his new surroundings with his senses of sight, touch, and feel.

From this early-established approach of exploration and discovery by the athlete, this method is continued with the more advanced pupils. The method includes four transitions -- the entry, drive, release, and recovery. Again, the instruction is kept to a minimum. The wholeness of each of these major transitions, as related to the whole stroke cycle, is stressed. This makes the coaching method much more simple and less detailed at this point.

The entry is a simple drop of the blade from the feathered position. This movement can be practiced while the novice is sitting at half slide. It is almost a natural movement for him to let the blade drop from the flat, feathered position. It is an easy relaxed drill for the novice.

The drive is a totally integrated motion of the trunk, legs and arms working together as a whole unit over the total length of the slide. Again, the feel of the body connected to the blade is important. Make sure the novice athlete takes time and does the drill slowly.

The release is the most detailed part of the instruction with the five Movements involved: the hands move down slightly, wrists break slightly, trunk moves a little through the perpendicular, knees break, and seat starts forward. All of these movements are done slowly initially, but eventually, quickly. So, the five Movements have the appearance of a single movement. Here, is where I began to learn to scull. It is the critical part of the cycle. A detail of the release in the shell is that the blade comes out slightly and then is feathered to forty-five degrees. Finally, the recovery is a trunk swing over the entire length of the shell. The swing is from the hips with the back straight, as stated earlier.

This instruction is minimal. Words are carefully selected and the importance of trying to see the whole is emphasized from the beginning. What you are trying to accomplish from the outset is that the athlete is being nudged into a more feeling mode of thinking. Thoughts become secondary. We are attempting to get the athlete close in his thoughts moving towards David Bohm's "Implicate Order." Thinking becomes non-thinking or intuitional. This is a non-conventional coaching approach. As I write, I can feel with my whole body the words that I am expressing. So too, I can feel the physical movements described on these pages.

The drills are simple for each of these transitions: quarter-slide front-end for the entry and the stationary drop of the blade into the water; a single stroke pull for the drive; quarter-slide back-end for the release; and full-slide set of the blade into the water at the entry at the end of the recovery. As was stated earlier, all of these transitions employ some part of the whole. Always, there is a relationship to the whole stroke. But really, in the beginning the drilling only has to utilize these five exercises. Later, we will add the controlled pause three inches off the body at the release.

With further advances in the skill acquisition, slow motion rowing or sculling can be introduced. This is where the sculler is encouraged to feel the movement of the whole, and the individual parts, to the stroke. He feels the trunk swing, and the movement of the whole leg action on the drive. By using slow motion learning of the skill, heightened consciousness is advanced. With Slow Motion, the sculler also approaches the Quantum level of this old art. He brings his thinking in line and conjoined, with the physical, his body and the shell. They all resonate together. George Wald states that, "Our growing scientific knowledge points unmistakably to the idea of a pervasive mind intertwined with and inseparable from the material universe. This thought may sound pretty crazy, but such thinking is

Specific Movement Phases

millennia old in the Eastern philosophies."[18] It is never so evident as when the sculler, in a highly concentrated fashion, is performing his slow motion sculling.

At this stage in the sculler's development, careful attention must be given to solid, continuous, tightly framed arm work. There is no rush to this component and it is well bonded to the blade depth and carriage off the water. Over the length of the drive, the arms should make a smooth transition from extension to flexion.

You are trying to do a minimum of instruction with maximum of participation by the athlete; having him experience more of this subtle level of moving. The consciousness is developed along with the skill. Intuition and attention develop; and the thought process shifts from the thinking mode to the feeling of sensations by the whole body. This fosters the mental state of *staying in the present*. It is the Now. "This emphasis on the now dictates a trust of what is really going on."[19] This is a completely different way of thinking. The analytical and mechanical, fragmented modes, are replaced by the instinctual, and the fluid, holistic modes of thought. Thus, thought and the material become one.

---

[18] George Wald, Nobel prize-winning biologist, *Cosmology of Life and Mind*, pp.10-11.
[19] Matthew Fox, *Meister Eckhart*, p.147

The Quantum Sculler

With this development, the athlete can now begin to be aware of his shell. He becomes more aware of the effect of his movements on the shell. He becomes more aware of his blades and the water. He begins to make his blade depth a quick, automatic placement and the extraction, a clean and swift movement to the feathered position.

Within these developments, the athlete is approaching another dimension along with his coach, the "Implicate Order." This fluid state must be lived inside and outside the shell. It is a fluid state! For this reason, all training must be accompanied with a daily visit to the training cushion for a meditation session. This must be promoted early in the process with the athlete. The mind must be as fluid as the body. It becomes a lifestyle, a higher order of consciousness, that we are all capable of accomplishing. This is where the training is reaching a much higher level of fluidity and wholeness. It does translate into a lightness and speed of movement of the shell.

Chapter Three - Integrated Drive and Release

> The Release - High Athleticism
> Fairbairn advised, "Sitting back there until the cows come home." Deliberation and exactness are keys. No rush. High Athleticism characterizes the release. The movements are subtle and silent, no clanging or banging of the oarlocks. Reactions are quick, fluid of motion, and intuitive. Fingers play an important role in both hands. Wrist action is minimized. Every move requires immediate succession of hands, trunk, and legs. The follow-through moves into the recovery. "All is in flux; nothing is stationary," proclaimed Heraclitus.
> - Jimmy Joy

Wholeness is in the total movement of the drive from the entry to the release. The movement integrates a very tight bonding between the whole body and the oars. There are no loose ends as the coordination between the trunk, legs, and arms is firm. The arm action has to be similar to the fluid action of the golfer's drive - one continuous movement. So the cycle eventually becomes one solid piece of continuous and simplistic motion. It is similar to the movement of a steady flowing stream. To maximize the athlete's strength, the total body must be relaxed and supple. The relaxation allows the athlete to move effectively and to use his power.

Visualize yourself at the entry, poised with an eager body and blade, ready to begin the drive. This flexible movement begins with arms, trunk, and legs totally involved and integrated. The entry position has the lower leg at a right angle to the gunwale and the legs are open at shoulder-width. This allows for the Core and the *Hara* to be open. At this apex position of the knees, the blade quickly enters the water. The trunk is angled towards the stern with the knees positioned below each armpit. The arms are spread in an open position that allows the heart to be open. A flexible trunk and hip action on the drive is imperative. The shoulders are relaxed. Head and shoulders remain level and eyes are fixed on the stern of the shell. During the drive phase, the legs are not rushed or hurried. They move with a steady, sequential pressure from the balls of the feet, from the calves to the thighs.

The pressure on the blade, on entry to the water, is constant and firm. Nothing is rushed and there is a steady flow of the whole movement towards the bow of the shell. At every point in this movement, each component of the arms, trunk, and legs are connected to the blade work. So it is a totally integrated action. The blade work is set at blade depth and remains in this position from the entry to the point of the release. With this ex-

Integrated Drive and Release

act positioning of the blade, the water is cupped and a depression is created behind the blade - the *Bernoulli Effect*. This positioning of the blade allows for an easy and clean exit from the water.

The legs go towards the midline of the body, as you go back on the drive, and move towards the armpits, as you come forward on the recovery. I refer to this as the "Butterfly Effect" with its fan-like motion of the legs. This tends to foster the connection between the legs, trunk, and arms. It is a rhythm action and not a simple push down. A masters sculler had this reaction to this new information: "Do the legs properly and you feel even better. Much more connection and I also think for some reason that it almost makes one have more uniform pressure on the blade face across the stroke cycle. When I was not proper with the legs, and then corrected it, I could feel it and see it in the stern." There is a rhythmic movement of the legs placed in two imaginary slots.

The trunk begins to open slightly in these early stages of the drive. This is the beginning of the trunk swing, the "Salt Shaker Effect", that carries through to the release of the blade from the water. The analogy of the "Salt Shaker Effect" approximates a person sitting at the dining table. He reaches forward from the hips with arms extended, takes the salt shaker and sits back. This backward swing from the hips combined with the forward swing from the hips is the foundation for achieving Flow.

See the 2014 Hobart College Crew in the foreground above, for a representation of the "salt shaker effect" in racing. Note that at half slide, the trunks are at the perpendicular position and there is ample leg action available for the second half of the drive.

In the drive, the legs carry the actions of the hips and the trunk, with the arms moving from extension to flexion back to extension in a fluid action over the length of the slide. The arm action is strongly reminiscent of the old cross saw work that was done by two men on the Douglas Fir trees in the Northwest. They worked continuously together in a harmonious rhythm of the arms.

These components of trunk, legs, and arms are all connected to the blade and remain continuously engaged from entry

Integrated Drive and Release

point to release with the subsequent arm and trunk follow-through movement. It is as though you are traversing a series of segments in the water with the trunk, legs, and arms all applying power through each of the segments. At the end of the drive, trunk and legs complete the movement together with arms trailing slightly. The trunk is positioned slightly beyond the perpendicular in the single and at the perpendicular in the quadruple scull. Throughout the movement, head and shoulders remain level. In sculling, both hands nudge the abdominal wall at the same level. Eyes are fixed on the stern of the shell. This becomes a unitary movement with these four components integrated and connected throughout this phase of the stroke. It is a tight, no-loose-ends arrangement. The mind remains in an empty or egoless state; it is relaxed. All components are cemented. If it is a multiple shell, the timing between the members must be precise to maximize the effect of the stroke cycle.

    The arms position for sweep rowing needs special consideration and attention. The rig is tight and narrow, so that the hands are positioned a little off center with a grip of two hand widths and a slightly bent inside arm. This allows for the pulling action to originate in both shoulders and the upper back muscles. This keeps the body over the keel line, which fosters more flow to the body. This ideal positioning of the hands is in stark contrast to the very wide grip, a wider rig and the hands positioned outside of the gunwale. This forces a much more severely bent inside arm, with the pulling action of the inside arm coming from the forearm, rather than the shoulder. The arms are significantly angled away from the trunk. This exaggerated placement of the arms also separates the position of the knees from the trunk. The simple drill for this movement is to do half-slide rowing at the front-end having your trunk move from leaning forward to sitting upright at the perpendicular at half-slide.

The precision trunk swing is the keystone for the whole stroke cycle. It falls on the legs to carry this system of trunk swing forward and backward on the slide. Thus, the legs function in a different way from the traditional approach of the legs "being the strongest part of your body, so apply them as quickly and hard as possible." The legwork is then more subtle, athletic and connected with the trunk and arms. Remember, the legs or legwork covers four purposes. First, legwork provides length to the stroke. Ned Hanlan discovered this over 100 years ago when he lengthened his track. Secondly, legs provide steady, even pressure through the balls of the feet during the drive. Third, the legs provide support and coordination for the work going on by the trunk and arms above the seat. Finally, legwork provides a steady controlled movement of the seat during the recovery.

In the traditional fragmented approach, movement on the drive is legs, then trunk and then arms. In contrast, the integrated method requires the development of a strong shoulder girdle because you feel the load immediately at the entry in the shoul-

Integrated Drive and Release

ders. Consciousness reaches profound levels as the athlete feels and is aware of the integral flow from the hips. The leg drive is a firm, steady flow from the entry to the release, and is connected with trunk, arms, and blade. The leg drive originates from the balls of the feet. Constant pressure is maintained on the balls of the feet throughout the drive. There are three transitions involved in the drive phase of the stroke:

- Arms and hands move silently and subtly from extension to flexion with little visible tension;
- The trunk moves from extension to a position of slight extension beyond the perpendicular at the release; and
- Legs move on the balls of the feet from a flexed position to an extended position at the end of the drive, finishing simultaneously with the trunk.

If you are starting the rank novice on the ergometer, then this is the only information that he needs to begin his rowing.

The completed picture is one of fine coordination, exquisite timing, and controlled integrated power. This is the centerpiece for the Flow quality in the stroke cycle and completes the picture of body, shell, and water being totally connected. The body rides completely over the keel line throughout the length of the drive. There is no deviation from this position, from the entry to the release. He sits with even pressure on both buttocks.

The Quantum Sculler

The pressure on the blade is established at the entry and remains constant throughout the drive phase. This means that the hands accelerate naturally. There is little need to point this out to the athlete. To begin, hands and fingers must have a light hold on the handles. Hands move down slightly as they approach the trunk wall. This creates an elliptical movement at the release. Wrists are flat, exerting power through the handle. Trunk and legs finish the drive phase of the stroke. They simultaneously form a 15-degree triangle beyond the perpendicular and serve as stabilizers for the arms coming in and out of bow. There is a nice flow from the elbows. In the rowing stroke, both hands perform the release, a "roll of the hands" release. Between the hands, there is no division of labor and consequently the release action is quiet. 2014vAny banging of the oar in the oarlock means that there is a heavy reliance on the inside wrist to release and a slight stopping of movement. You don't want these characteristics in the cycle. The sculler continues to sit, with even pressure on the buttocks, looking forward toward the stern.

Concentration was intense, as I began to get a feel for the movement. The Release is the critical connection from the end of the Drive and the beginning of the Recovery. It is an important transition that must be perfected and essentially very fluid.

Integrated Drive and Release

Pictured above is the author in the 1980's at Craftsbury Sculling Camp. Take particular note of:

- The firmness of the legs.
- The solid angle formed by the trunk and legs.
- The angled position of the arms.
- The level hands.
- The trunk is erect and slightly beyond the perpendicular.
- The trunk finishes with the legs.
- The trim of the shell as the bow cuts the water.
- The fluid release.
- The release angle of the blades from the water.

The Quantum Sculler

    A recent trip to the canal to watch the local college crews found me treated to a large "clunking" noise at the completion of each stroke. This was not complex, rather it was simply a pronounced move from one edge of the oar sleeve to another. This was performed by the severe drop from the horizontal position of the inside wrist. I explained to the coach that this action should be quieter and continuous, without the pause at the end of each stroke. The release has to become a deliberate two-stage move to quarter, out of the water and then feather. The wrist action must be less severe and much more subtle, with the handle moving to the fingers. More complex than what the crew is presently doing. The "clunking" is an indicator that there is a pause in the cycle and the crew is hesitating in the follow-through, without continuity on the whole. It also represents a loss of a fraction of a second. These fractions add up over the course of the race. The coach was receptive and immediately introduced the idea to the crew. It will take some time to move along the Complexity/Consciousness band of Evolution for these crews. Too much is ingrained. The coach has to be more knowledgeable and able to execute this refined movement himself. He has to get in the single shell and learn the stroke.

Integrated Drive and Release

Bob Pearce racing in Vancouver, B.C.

Take note of the relaxed arms and the splay of his legs during the drive. His legs have ample room for more movement during the second half of the drive. He has an integrated drive combining the legs, trunk and arms. Also, notice his relaxed facial expression, with a hint of a smile. The Bernoulli Effect with his blade action is also displayed.

The late Claude Saunders, a former clubmate of Pearce's remarked at the time, "watching him row, you'd swear he wasn't pulling, but he never pulled a weak stroke in his life He made it look effortless". Pearce indeed was noted for his smooth

The Quantum Sculler

sculling technique and uncanny ability in keeping his boat running between strokes. In single sculling this is of crucial importance. The primary components of the rowing stroke are the blade entry and extraction, as well as the movement of the trunk up the slide prior to the initiation of a new stroke. These must be accomplished in a smooth, yet efficient, manner in order to minimize the disruptive influences or "check" on the run of the shell. Thus, the blade entry or "catch" must be smooth yet quick enough so that valuable boat speed is not lost between strokes. The extraction of the blade must be accomplished in a similar manner. Pearce had apparently mastered these aspects of the stroke: "There wasn't a wasted movement in his stroke. Once he put the blades at the catch, it was a full stroke from that moment through. Moreover, his bladework at the finish of the stroke was perhaps his strongpoint. He did not drop his wrist and roll his blade out, like most scullers do. He rolled it in his fingers. His hands were so big, he dropped his wrist a very little bit and then rolled the blade in his fingers, which no one else could do."[20]

This critical section of the stroke cycle parallels the follow-through motions of golf, baseball, and tennis swings. The end of the drive and the beginning of the recovery movements are in a one-to-one ratio. This permits the movement of the hands and

---

[20] William Paul Beedling, *Henry Robert "Bob" Pearce, A Biography*

Integrated Drive and Release

arms to slide easily from the drive phase into the recovery phase of the stroke cycle. The release and follow-through are so critical for the continued wholeness quality of the total movement. So this must be mastered over many miles of practice. Lower rate work and slow motion rowing is extremely helpful in achieving this mastery. The five movements that appear to be one movement are: the hands move downward slightly, the wrists break a little, the arms are extended, the trunk moves through the perpendicular, and the knees rise a little. Again the movement of the arms comes from the elbows. The blade is positioned at blade depth when the release begins. The hands move downward slightly, moving the blade to a quarter out of the water. At this point, the feathering of the blade begins. The blade is released from the water at a forty-five degree angle to the water's surface. So it is an efficient, elliptical motion, not a squared action. The blade does not come fully out of the water before the feather is done. The angle of the trunk at the release is important for supporting the release action and follow-through. Both the trunk and the legs serve as stabilizers for the movement of the hands and arms. The athlete remains momentarily in an open position, as he draws the handles to the body in an unhurried action of the strong arm draw. He sits tall with his body orientation upward. This keeps the weight off the bow and allows the bow deck to remain level. He must visualize the bow running level. Again, flow of the movement at this point in the cycle is very athletic. This flow of the drive is congruent with the run of the shell. It is a perfect match. It is during this phase the breath is inhaled, distending the stomach at the release. Power is carefully applied with the 90% law operating, where you only apply 90% effort. Any more pressure than this wastes your power, produces strain and anxiety. This rule applies with all rates of striking. You follow the old adage, *"Pull what you can handle."* In a similar vein, the former East German rowing literature stated that you should not try to pull too much or too little. The stroke then can be viewed as a whole. We are totally connected to the shell, oars and water. We should view the body as a solid entity from the toes to the crown of your head. No loose parts! The speed of the release is a critical movement for raising the stroke rate. You have to become comfortable with doing three times twenty strokes at a high rate for thirty seconds. Every stroke has to be recalled in the sculler's mind and evaluated for cleanness and precision. This becomes an exercise in Mindfulness. The preferable practice is to return to the same starting point and to do these high pieces at the end of a workout. Eventually, the rushed movements of the release become less hurried. This is still a vivid memory of controlled transition for me. The drill for the release is quarter-slide back-end continuous sculling. All of these drills engage a significant part of the stroke that is a

Integrated Drive and Release

reflection of the whole stroke. Bohm referred to this reality as the hologram or holo-movement. Thus, this body is a small universe operating as a hologram. The movement of the entry is contained throughout the whole of this moving body, in the legs, feet, trunk, and arms. This is not a body governed by words such as prepare and set. This is a continuous moving body, "dancing," in the shell. The body flows with every component engaged as part of the whole movement. The sculler's mind remains fixed in the present.

It is also important to detail the state of the body during this phase. It is relaxed and "pulling what the athlete can handle comfortably," no straining, fluid. The total relaxation of the body, the trunk, the legs, the arms, and the facial features is what eliminates anxiety, allows the body to coordinate and move effectively and ultimately to generate more power. The detail of these two important parts to the stroke cycle is so critical for the smooth flow of the Movements and the subsequent smooth flow of the shell.

Chapter Four - Active Recovery and Sculler's Entry

The Entry

The body is well positioned over the keel line. Legs are firm and shoulders and trunk high with good reach from the shoulders. Knees are splayed, the heart opened wide. The sculler is poised on the balls of the feet. The Blade drops in with the whittling move -- it simply disappears. Highly skilled fingers perform. There is a subtle and fluid transition from recovery to drive. Now the whole body engages to begin this power phase.

- Jimmy Joy

On the Release, the oar handle is held between the roots of the fingers and the pad of the hand with the wrist flat. This whole action of the Release is completed as a single, quick and relaxed movement. It is highly athletic. Again, similar to the Entry, it is an unconscious, reflexive motion. Between these two movements, the Entry and the Release, completed with skill, accuracy, and consistency, lies our ability to develop Flow at every opportunity.

The Old Coach, Bob Fitzpatrick, would always describe the Release as having the wrists perfectly flat, but his physical demonstration displayed arched wrists. This was his method of releasing the blade from the water with the wrists arched. Fitzpatrick related that the champion sculler Robert Pearce, with whom he enjoyed a two-year coaching relationship, would simply spin the blade into place at the Release and Entry by tapping the scull handles with his large fingers, while keeping his wrists flat. These two methods are to be regarded as personal.[21]

Lindsey Hochman, a USA International Sculler, recently exclaimed, "Timing is everything in sculling." This is particularly true for the Recovery, the Active Recovery. This precision timing reaches full development during the winter months with the employment of daily simulation exercises done without the oar handle on the ergometer. In the spring, this produces exquisite timing that is evident the first day on the water with the perfectly balanced shell. This intricate timing involves the movement of the seat and the movement of the trunk. There is no setting of the body angle out of the bow position. The angle of the trunk changes throughout the recovery. The trunk has to travel in a larger arc than the movement of the seat, but they arrive together at the entry point of the blade. The end product is a beautiful pairing of these two movements - the farthest reach of the seat and the well-postured extended trunk. This timing is something that can be practiced on land, on the ergometer with-

---

[21] William Paul Beedling, *Henry Robert "Bob" Pearce, A Biography*

out the oar handle, or, by placing one foot on a bench or chair and swing forward from the hips as you move your butt forward.

The movement of the trunk and seat out of bow, begins with the movements of the release and follow-through. The hands are relaxed with most of the responsibility for making the movement of the release falling to the fingers. The movements of the fingers are so deft and subtle. In the rowing stroke, both hands are involved with the rolling movements of the fingers and the handle. There is very little wrist action employed as the arms move to the straight-arm position and the trunk moves slightly through the perpendicular. At this point, the knees start to rise and the seat moves towards the stern. The body also moves with the utmost agility and nimbleness. These five movements are the critical initial action out of the bow. The movements are performed so quickly in sequence that they look like a singular movement.

Thus, the Recovery becomes a perfected example of quantum physicist David Bohm's "Implicate Order" where everything at the subatomic level is connected, the arms, legs and trunk. Everything is seamless and whole. This action is continuous, the trunk moving with the seat, from just in front of the perpendicular line, to the eventual position at full-slide. The trunk moves a little, the seat moves a little, always towards the stern. There is equal pressure on both buttocks throughout this

Active Recovery and Sculler's Entry

recovery phase, with the body moving perfectly over the keel in both sculling and sweep rowing. This keeps the hull running perfectly level. These actions of the trunk and the seat are entwined and are the beginning of Flow in the shell. The eyes focus on a level of about three feet above the stern deck and fifty feet beyond the stern. This allows the sculler to see the stern clearly. By focusing on the stern, he "watches" for any dipping of the bow or any side-to-side wiggle.

Paul Fuchs, an accomplished competitive sculler and a six-time USA Lightweight Champion, describes the idea of the foot floating in the shoe. When there is no pressure on the footplate, there is no pressure on the top of the shoe either. There is no pulling on your toes to get to the catch. The shell simply runs forward or slides under you and the body almost remains in one place. These movements are done with complete efficiency. There is definitely a hidden restfulness at work here between strokes. The shell is allowed to flow under the body" with minimal effort." Some coaches feel that this is the stage when races are won and lost. The mind rests as well, with no stress or hurry to its nature. At this point, the consciousness of the sculler has dominion over the physical, especially with the precision of his timing. He experiences a far different reality than the ordinary person who is attempting to scull.

The athlete should sit lightly on the seat throughout the recovery. The trunk should be erect, so that he is sitting

The Quantum Sculler

with proper torso height. This is good alignment and posture as outlined earlier. The trunk swing and the seat movement forward are where the mind and matter really come together. You have to feel both the movement from the hips and the movement of the seat going forward on the track. They arrive together at the front end. Sit on the seat with even pressure on the sit bones of both cheeks. We would say, "The wind whistles under your butt." Sitting lightly on the seat allows the shell to run out further, so the relaxed body during the recovery only moves a little. The shell slides through the water. The hands and knuckles rise slightly as you near full-reach. Shoulders will remain level during the final stages of the movement, assisted by letting the hands move up slightly from the toes-position to full reach, bringing the blade closer to the water, preventing the trunk from pitching. The seat, trunk, and blade arrive at full extension simultaneously. This is proper seat/body timing.

    The trunk swing is the foundation of the Stroke Cycle, the keystone in the arch of skill. He should really feel the movement of the hips forward and backward. It is the muscles of the hips that control the movement of the seat on the recovery. Steve Fairbairn wrote, "All races are won by the crew with the best forward swing." [22] In performing the stroke, the consistent posi-

---

[22] Steve Fairbairn, *Some Secrets of Successful Rowing*, p. 267

Active Recovery and Sculler's Entry

tioning of the hands, arms, trunk legs and blade at the entry and the consistent positioning of the same at the release, is the basis for rhythm. The trunk swing serves the same purpose as a metronome. The extent of the stroke length is tight and uniform. So, it is safe to say that this is the most critical portion of the stroke cycle.

This hip movement is in phase with the run of the shell on the drive. The leg action should be steady, smooth and splayed shoulder-width during the swing forward, allowing enough room for the stomach. The stomach becomes distended as you move forward on the recovery and requires some space. Otherwise, it will press against the thighs shortening the stroke length. The sculler's body becomes part of Nature, part of the shell running under him. There is no separation between him and the external world of the seat and slide. It is an all-encompassing feeling and state of being. The specific details of the recovery require that the seat move a little when the trunk moves a little over the full course of the slide so that the body and seat arrive together at full reach. The knees end up perpendicular to the gunwales and splayed. The trunk is extended from the hips.

On the recovery, the blade is carried slightly off the water to full extension. Olympian Conn Findlay wrote the following in 1971, "rigging up to strike the catch is wrong and the East Germans are proving it. If you look at some pictures of them you will notice that they never lift the blades more than a couple of inches off the water. There isn't any striking down on the water. As Karl Adam said in Berkeley, 'why hit a swinging door with a sledge hammer.' The catch must be firm and deliberate and with a minimum of missed water in order to move the boat, remembering that the boat will move backwards if the man moves without having a hold of the water." This is very sound advice from this multiple medal winner, who was coached by George Pocock. From the author Dr. Ernst Herberger, "The crucial prerequisite for fast entry is a late and quick squaring of the blades. Simultaneous with the squaring, the blades should be brought close to water, so as to enter by the shortest route possible."[23]

At full extension of the arms and trunk, the knuckles rise slightly followed by the pulling action and the raising of the wrists to execute the squaring action. The downward movement of the blade and the pulling action of the blade must be quick and done together. There is much less missing of water compared to having the blade prominently squared above the water, pause, then placed into the water in a deliberate but slow fashion. You have to feel the blade in your hands. At each end of the slide, the hands must be continually moving. This is an important ingredient for developing flow. Any large gap in these two movements is evident. Throughout the recovery, the trunk

---

[23] Dr. Ernst Herberger, *The GDR Text of Oarsmanship*, p.73.

Active Recovery and Sculler's Entry

and legs are relaxed. It is in this part of the stroke that the sculler calms himself, eliminating any anxieties as he moves forward.

The hands and knuckles rise slightly as you near full-reach. Shoulders will remain level during the final stages of the movement, assisted by letting the hands move up slightly from the toes-position to full reach, bringing the blade closer to the water, preventing the trunk from pitching. The seat, trunk, and blade arrive at full extension simultaneously. This is proper seat/body timing. At the entry, the seated position has the trunk pitched forward and elongated from the hips; the arms are slightly angled downward from the shoulders; the knees are situated in the armpits; the feet are poised on the balls; the hands are relaxed with finger control; and the head and eyes are fixated over the stern of the shell. The position of the body at the entry has the armpits over the knees with trunk in a relaxed elongated state and the lower legs are perpendicular to the gunwales. With this detailed position, the body is extremely compact and ready to spring out of the front-end. It is momentarily poised. The sculler's thoughts parallel the connections of the Implicate Order and are focused on the deep, deep feelings of the body action, where everything is integrated with the blades and the water. This transition from the end of the recovery to the beginning of the drive must be smooth and whole. This involves the follow-through of the arms. With these qualities firmly in place in the cycle, the motion becomes effortless and timeless. At this point, the athlete is approaching a much higher level of consciousness as his focus becomes stronger and he is able to remain in the present.

Remaining in the present, is really the key for a good entry movement. This movement is finished with a fluid movement of the trunk into the armpits combined with quick blade work. So, the entry is the key to getting into the Flow State. The sculler simply keeps repeating the quality of the entry movements, both blade and trunk actions. This is really the focus for the experienced sculler -- the movement into the entry, the entry itself, and the initial movement of the drive. With the quick entry, you feel the immediate stress on your shoulder girdle. It is a bell note that must be experienced for each stroke. The entry movements become a state of mind and body. They are one, a complete organism.

All of this produces a solid and balanced platform in the shell to execute the Entry. Attention must be given to this body position for the proper execution of the Entry. Too often, it is overlooked with the preoccupation of the movement of the blade. The stern deck remains level and poised with these accurate and polished movements. This sets up a powerfully positioned whole body of legs, trunk and arms at the full-reach position. In the rowing stroke, the arms are angled down below the shoulders and slightly lateral. The inside arm is bent a little and the outside knee is in the outside armpit. In sweep rowing the hands

Active Recovery and Sculler's Entry

holding the handle are spread about 5-6 inches apart. Both legs are firmly placed symmetrical to the keel line. Firm legs are the foundation of the stroke. The angle of the legs is critical. Do not have the seat too close to the foot stretchers. Too much compression of the legs leads to a weak leg drive. Well-positioned legs provide a strong relationship between trunk and arms at the entry. They are coupled. It is important that the coach monitors this detail very closely. This is assisted by the narrower two-hand width separation of the hands on the handle. The weight of the oar is on the hands from the release to the toes position and the weight shifts to the blade from the toes to full reach.

  The Entry blade work is simply a point on the continuous process. It is a reflexive movement. The actual rhythmic movement of the hand, knuckle, and wrist is continuous and has a micro flow quality to it. The hands on the handle must be relaxed to achieve this action. Very light work with the fingers is necessary. The fingers are totally relaxed, which allows the handles to be positioned further out on the fingers. This also facilitates the finger action of the entry. This positions the hands with a slight depression in the wrists just before the entry actions - the movement of the knuckles towards the body and the raising of the wrists, the "whittling action". There is no preparation of the blade position. It begins when the feathered blade reaches its furthest reach. As the hands rise, the knuckles rise slightly above the wrists and the wrists have a slight depression in their position. This relaxes the wrists and sets up the ensuing movements of the entry. At this point in the stroke, the knuckles complete the recovery by slightly rising. With the knuckles rising slightly, the blade simply drops into the water. It drops from the feather at a slight angle to the water surface with assistance from the relaxed fingers. You begin to pull with your fingers and raising your wrists simultaneously. The blade squares to the water in the water. It is a "sleight of hand trick." In the words of sculling coach Frank Cunningham, [24] this is a "wood whittling," [25] the movement between the knuckles and wrists with the wrists going to the flat pulling position. As the hands rise, the knuckles rise slightly above the wrists and the wrists have a slight depression in their position. This relaxes the wrists and sets up the ensuing movements of the entry. At this point in the stroke, the knuckles complete the recovery by slightly rising. With the knuckles rising slightly, the blade simply drops into the water. It drops from the feather at a slight angle to the water surface with assistance from the relaxed fingers. You begin to pull with your fingers and raising your wrists simultaneously. The blade squares to the water in the water. The blade action is simply an instinctive movement done with skilled quickness.

---

[24] Frank Cunningham was a Harvard Graduate, a school teacher, and was coached by Bert Haines, an old Thames River Waterman. Cunningham coached the sculler's entry.
[25] "Wood Whittling" is performed by a small knife on a piece of wood. You draw the hand/knife towards the body from the wrists.

Active Recovery and Sculler's Entry

The drop is not a vertical drop, but curvilinear, with the lower edge leading into the water. The blade goes to blade depth. It is at this point, that the blade is squared and the pull begins. There is a slight separation between the drop of the blade and the pulling action. This allows water to gather on the blade. These movements can be illustrated on land with your hand placed palm up in front of your body (See illustration of the hands at the end of this chapter). Or, simply take the little finger and move it downward with the whole palm following.

At this point there is a quick reversal of the body movement from the Recovery to the Drive. It is merely "a blink of the eye." This is the simple anatomy of the Entry. If you start to pull before the blade is fully buried, you will have a white water splay effect on the front face of the blade. It is a just a matter of a fraction of a second, within which to have the blade fully and quickly covered, followed by the pulling action. It is important that swift entry of the blade be combined with swift power application. It is a two-cycle movement, the drop and the pull.

The Quantum Sculler

Here is a young Bobby Pearce, pictured above. Note the deep cavity with his port scull. This is the Bernoulli Effect. It is much easier to achieve if the entry movements begins with the blade in the horizontal position. The water is quickly cupped by the twin actions of the vertical movement to blade depth, quickly followed by the horizontal pull. Of course, the fingers play a huge role in applying these two important movements. This is in stark contrast to the conventional squaring of the blade above the water's surface, then the blade enters the water and the pull occurs -- a three-component movement. It is more difficult to obtain accuracy with your blade placement doing the entry this way.

Active Recovery and Sculler's Entry

With this conventional approach, the beginner is encouraged and prodded to make an early squaring action of the blade, then place it with a deliberate action into the water and then pull. This action in comparison to the sculler's movement is slow, more time-consuming, and mechanical. It leads to a definite pausing of the blade above the water. This instruction is more elaborate and serial in nature. There is too much instruction and not enough doing by the sculler. With this approach, the critique of the movements is continued until a perceived perfection is achieved. It is perfection in inefficiency. It does fit in nicely with fragmented linear physics. This method is totally concerned with the blade action and there is no addressing of the body position and movement at the entry. It is a serious oversight when only the blade action, the squaring above the water, is addressed.

With the two-component action, both a movement and time are saved. The blade should simply disappear from the recovery position. As the sculler advances, he begins to feel that his hands are the blades and the blades are his hands. He also takes his entry to another level, when he concentrates on achieving the Bernoulli Effect immediately. The Entry simply becomes the grip of the water with the blade at blade depth. It becomes a single component action, when the horizontal is quickly combined with the horizontal motion. It is important that from 3/4 slide to full-slide, that the weight on the handle shifts to the

The Quantum Sculler

blade and the blade drops in. As you move from 3/4 to full slide, there develops a slight depression in the wrists that facilitates the squaring action of the blade. It is also critical that the seat slows down as you approach the front-stops to ensure that trunk movement begins slightly before the seat. This has to be drilled and drilled. Eventually the two movements start together. Sculling coach, Mike Wagner wrote recently, "it is interesting how it can feel like the blade just gets sucked into the water to proper blade depth, pitch, and load all with barely any effort to rotate the oar in the hands. Let the water do the work."

The two anatomical trigger points in the cycle include the knees feeling placement in the armpits at the entry and the thumbs nudging the abdominal wall at the release. This is where the transitions occur. When the blade is squared in the water, the third knuckle line is placed along the extreme inside edge of the handle, so that the fingers are relaxed and in a strong pulling position. This is a very quick reflexive action that parallels the action of the release. It is important that the swift entry of the blade be combined with swift power application -- a speedy coupling of two actions. This "whittling" movement of the knuckles and the wrists should be simulated on land until it becomes ingrained. The sculler should also visualize this action of the fingers, knuckles and the wrists. Again, relaxed and subtle fingers play a major role in making this action. The blade should simply disappear from the recovery position or the blade simply slips into the water.[26] Recently, the Hobart Crew Coach, Paul Bugenhagen, related how a parent of one of his oarsmen, in taking photos of the crew, could never capture the blades squared above the water. The same is true of old pictures of Ned Hanlan. Either the blade is feathered or in the water.

This entry leads to silent arms and steady leg pressure during the drive, so the movement is whole and integrated from the shoulders and toes to the blade. There is even pressure on the balls of the feet. Arms transition fluidly from the straight and silent position to one of relaxed flexion at the release. Arms are a complete unit with trunk, legs, and blade. Silent arms really help in leveling the shell on the drive, rather than the shell experiencing a "porpoising" effect.

---

[26] From Vince Reynolds: You know I was speaking to Richard MacFarlen on this subject yesterday. He was watching our 4x and 2x race and he said it was crazy to watch me, and then the others. He said the blade slipped into the water. Nothing missed and I looked effortless.

The Quantum Sculler

The entry under the Fitzpatrick/Pearce method is actually a slight lift from the hips, with the arms on it over the course of the drive - the "salt shaker". Again, it is important to understand the fine movements with the hands and fingers. This detail, or coaching with detail in mind, is very important for the education of both the coach and the athlete. The skill development leads the coach and athlete to a new level of consciousness, and a higher state of relaxation. The coach must be adept at demonstrating the movements. He must remain athletic throughout his coaching career.

You must be relaxed in the fingers to perform this exquisite skill. You must also sit relaxed on the seat, with an erect trunk, throughout the recovery phase leading to the entry. You must sit lightly. My hope is for the sculler, following reading this section, to then be able to go out and perform this entry skill with some degree of competence.

Active Recovery and Sculler's Entry

Ernest James Barry (1882–1968) was a British rower and Thames Waterman, five times Professional Sculling World Champion during the early part of the 20th century. Note the relaxed handhold and the position of the third set of knuckles, as well as the flat, slightly depressed, wrists. His blades are squared into the water at this point. It is his relaxed fingers on the handle that allows him to "whittle" the handle at each end of the track. This whittling action squares and feathers the blade. George

The Quantum Sculler

Pocock's father, Aaron, thought that Barry was one of the finest scullers of his time and that George should attempt to copy his technique.

Lower Edge Sculling

The Blade is carried close to the water. Once the blade reaches full extension, the stern edge moves down to the water with a rhythmic movement of the hands/knuckles. Slightly raise the hands and knuckles, start to pull the handle towards you, letting the blade into the water. It is so simple, quick, and immediate, with no square blade above the water. You see the blade on the horizontal one moment and then it disappears. You save a movement by not squaring the blade above the water. This should be simulated on land with your hand repeated often. The rhythmic movement of the hand, knuckle and wrist is actually a continuous and flowing action. The hands on the handle, the fingers, must be relaxed to achieve this action.

The drills for the Recovery are similar to the drills for the Entry. You do parts of the Recovery to Entry from three quarter, half, quarter, and zero slide starting positions. However, you always should be thinking and feeling the wholeness in the stroke cycle.

Active Recovery and Sculler's Entry

The one weight lifting exercise that should be done on a regular basis is the Composite. The athlete stands on a bench and lowers the weight below the level of the bench. Then the athlete does a full clean action with the bar. This exercise will strengthen the shoulders that are necessary for the integral entry where the legs, arms, and trunk are involved simultaneously.

The Entry is the heart and soul of the Stroke. It is what makes this Stroke Cycle so unique and unorthodox. In sculling, we have to use the natural gift of our hands and fingers on the scull handles. It is almost a mystical action. Nature has bestowed this great gift, not our wrists or forearms, but the skilled use of our hands and fingers. It deserves our total attention directed towards a light touch with the fingers.

R.C. Lehman who wrote the classic, *The Complete Oarsman* over 100 years ago, admired Ned Hanlan, and had this to say about the incomparable sculler and his entry, "His sculling was distinguished by extraordinary length and power, qualities which he secured, not merely by a remarkable suppleness, but by the perfect combination of body and legs for his work in the water. He seized his beginning decisively and instantly by the prompt application of bodyweight. His body and slide movements blend into one."[27] These comments are extremely appropriate for the modern sculler in his approach to the Entry.

---

[27] R.C Lehman, *The Complete Oarsman*, p 49

The Quantum Sculler

    Today before practice, while having my daily cup of morning tea, I thought of the entry and how Old Coach Fitzpatrick taught it and I was mystified. Rowing peers in the St. Catharines boathouse would enquire how I achieve the wonderful Entry and I would respond that I don't know. Subsequently, wherever and whenever I sculled, people would comment on my beautiful, athletic, Entry. I could not remember Fitz working on the Entry, except to say, let the blade drop into the water. Well, this morning, while sitting and reflecting, it finally came to me after 60 years. Fitz worked extensively on the release. I did come to realize over the course of those years that the Entry was the inverse movement of the Release. Fitzpatrick, interestingly enough, never said anything directly about the Entry, nothing in great detail. He simply said to drop the blade into the water, when the chest arrives at the knees. The blade just disappeared into the water from the horizontal position. It happened because his description of the release was so detailed and precise from his direct coaching. This is how he achieved precision at the entry. At Wesleyan, some of my best athletes, in viewing my sculling, stated that the blade simply disappeared. You can really feel the water on the blade with the quicker entry movement. You feel it in the shoulders initially. The Entry comes with a great amount of engagement by the fingers and the lats, then the legs. I did add my own perspective in those years on the importance of the finger action, the light touch. So I always consid-

Active Recovery and Sculler's Entry

ered the entry mystical because you cannot see it as you can the release. I still feel that way today.

Fitz always had you work at full-slide. There was never any part-stroke work. So, he was always working on the whole. Even though I do like working at half and quarter slide, it is important that we continue to think about the whole stroke. We should have the athlete think or imagine with the whole in mind. The effective drill for this is 1/4 slide sculling at the back-end, where you are doing clean releases or the clean, quick, disappearing entries. This is what we should be teaching our juniors and our novices. It is much easier for them than some linear, Newtonian and elaborate scheme for taking the entry. You have two components: the quick drop of the blade, the vertical component, quickly followed by the pull of the blade, the horizontal component. These two moves must come together very quickly.

Fitzpatrick had it figured out through his wisdom. He had worked with English orthodoxy; he had coached the undefeated Bob Pearce (actually it is his entry); and he had witnessed Fairbairn stroke with the English crew at the 1932 Olympics. Fitz then came up with his own synthesis of these three methods. It has remained, over these many years, a very effective and modern scientific approach to the sculling stroke. I feel he was doing the Quantum, without realizing he was doing it. Certainly his leadership style was that way. He treated me as a peer.

The Quantum Sculler

This I carried over into my own coaching, whether I was dealing with juniors, college or International athletes.

The result is a finger-pressure entry where the blade simply disappears from the horizontal and the entry simply becomes a transition phase from the recovery to the drive, so that the stroke is whole at this point.

The coach, in a subtle way, begins his instruction by ingraining into the novice sculler an appreciation of smooth movements and the extensive use of his fingers on the handle. His approach is a totally integrative method where he presents the whole movement from the beginning of his instructions to the novice. The sculler's entry is extremely easy for the beginner to learn.

Sculling Coach Mike Wagner has this to add on instructing novice scullers, "*The Quantum Sculler* text has a direct relationship on how to teach novice scullers as well. The idea of simplicity of movement can make the sport more accessible for beginners. Here at the *Sagamore Rowing Association*, I have been teaching the scullers entry for the past four years and I am pleased to note that the feedback from the athletes has been overwhelmingly positive. I start from day one with a new sculler by teaching then to skim the blade on the water when feathered and then use a minimal action with the fingers for the blade entry. The result is that the scullers learn to keep their hands at a consistent height, so the shell is more stable. The scullers can feel

Active Recovery and Sculler's Entry

the blade hook in and begin to grip the water at near full compression. It is a very natural way to teach sculling.

They do it as a natural course of placing the blade into the water. They simply come forward on the slide and, at the last fraction of a second, execute a simple drop of the blade into the water. Their blade may be slightly under squared, but this doesn't matter. As time passes, they will gain ever more speed at placing the blade. Little has to be said to the neophyte at this point. All of this is done in one simple motion, the under square, the entry of the blade into the water, and the pulling action. The young sculler completes the movement as an integrated and single movement. Eventually, he will get the blade squared in the water. However, there is a flow to the movement and it is continuous in a rough sort of way. The critical point is to keep the blade moving at the entry with no significant pause of the blade above the water's surface."

Specific drills for the novice sculler include the following:

- First, sit at a slide position where the athlete is most comfortable, see the level hands, feel the even seat pressure and foot pressure, feel the symmetry and wholeness as the sculler quickly drops the blade into the water;
- Secondly, swing from the hips from the hands-position (three inches off the body) to full reach - feel the oneness of the movement of the trunk, and the sculls;

- Third, sit at the release and feel the wholeness of arms and trunk as you release the blade slightly from the water;
- Fourth, sit at full slide (comfortable position) with blade at blade depth and begin the drive with the legs, trunk, and arms together. Apply pressure evenly throughout the whole drive and complete the movement with the legs and trunk together; with the arms trailing slightly.

All of these drills are completed with a sense of wholeness and non-fragmentation. Slowly, over time, the details of the individual movements will be addressed by coach and sculler.

The visual focus is on the even level of the hands and the mental focus is a present awareness of the knees sliding into and out of the armpits. This combines unified body and mind with the whole athletic environment. Both aspects are present. So the entry is a unified effort.

Vince Reynolds sent this e-mail to me regarding his entries and releases: "Last night I was again able to recreate that effect I was talking about; where in sitting nice and tall, I mean taller than you think, at each end of the slide and focusing upon the stern and feeling the velocity of the shell, so as to gain a vision of when the velocity is just ready to drop off, then change direction. Well, the shell just goes and goes and goes and then the best part. As you say, think of the blades as your hands and your hands as the blades; and all of a sudden it is like I am see-

Active Recovery and Sculler's Entry

ing my entries, my releases, my blades just inches off the water and the shell ready to lift off and float away. I can keep this going for now at least 500 meters before the spell breaks. However, I now know I can recreate this. The entries were swift and I felt almost zero load as compared to the heavy-effort loading like we see (and I usually feel) when we watch the videos from the world-class fellows. I am finally starting to get fewer water drops on the foredeck, when this effect is in play."

Drills for the entry include:

- Continuous sculling at the front quarter of the slide;
- Placement drills from three quarter, half, quarter and zero slide as starting points, back-chaining from three quarter slide. This is where you move from three quarter slide to full slide and place the blade in the water quickly and then extract the blade and move back to three quarter slide position. When you become more accomplished with the drill, you can carry the blade off the water surface.
- Finally, there is the 3-pause drill. Pause, 3 inches off the body, pause at 3/4 slide forward, pause with blade in water at full-reach, and pull to 3 inches off the body position.

Columbia Lightweights with blades close to the water, ready to make the sculler's entry.

An effective drill, that former six-time USA National Sculling Champion, Paul Fuchs, used on a day when he was too tired to train or the water was too rough, was to find a quiet spot and work with one oar at a time. He would watch the entry and learn and feel how the blade wanted to go into the water. Then, he would do the same for the finish. He would do this many, many strokes at a time. He would just sit there and go around in circles, with his eyes closed, until he could feel exactly what the

Active Recovery and Sculler's Entry

blade wanted to do going into the water. He would then try to feel the same sensation while rowing. [28]

Lindsey Hochman, former USA Quadruple Sculler asks, "Why would you carry the blade so far off the water? With this entry, the blade can be carried very close to the surface of the water. And, with this entry, the young novice naturally carries the blade close to the water or on it." This helps with shell balance and allows for quick entry into the water. Again, the relaxed, subtle fingers play a major role in making this action. Tight hold of the fingers on the handle is destructive for any attempts to complete this subtle entry. This can be achieved with the novice sculler. This places relaxed hands and fingers, with wrists flat and elongated, in a poised state. The hands follow the handle to the entry. With the fingers controlling the handle, power goes through the handle efficiently, rather than into the handle, when the grip is tight and palmed. It is similar to a monkey hanging from a limb.

The question might be asked about blade height and what does the athlete do in rough water. I remember following a Yale 150 crew on the Housatonic River. When they turned a bend in the river and were faced with rough conditions, they immediately feathered and carried the blades higher off the water. The adjustment came automatically.

---

[28] Correspondence from Paul Fuchs in May 2014.

The Quantum Sculler

Not only drilling on parts of the stroke cycle can help development, but also coaching intensive sessions over 1,500 meters. A section of the river or lake is staked out, where the coach stops and checks the athlete's individual faults. Then he turns the crew around and goes back over the 1,500 meters doing the same, stopping and checking. You keep doing this for 60 to 90 minutes. Not much mileage, but ample intensity of effort and concentration is involved. This practice is good to do at various times of the training year. It really helps to foster development of technical skills.

A final note on the anatomical pinpoints, there are two:

- At the entry, the knees are in the armpits and the blade should be in the water. In sweep rowing make sure that the outside armpit is over the knee, otherwise the outside shoulder will drop and the shoulders will twist downwards rather that remaining horizontal.
- Secondly, the thumbs just nudge the abdominal wall at the release of the blade from the water.

So the limits of the stroke are clearly defined by the feel of the anatomy, the knees and armpits at the entry, and the thumbs and wall of the stomach at the release.

Active Recovery and Sculler's Entry

Hand Simulations of the Entry Movements.

It is a little rhythmic movement of the hand and knuckles. Raise the hands slightly, raise the wrists and start the pull, letting the blade drop into the water.

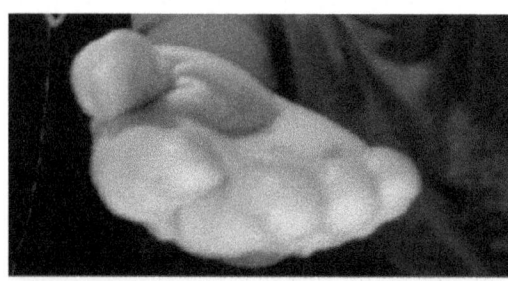

Recovery

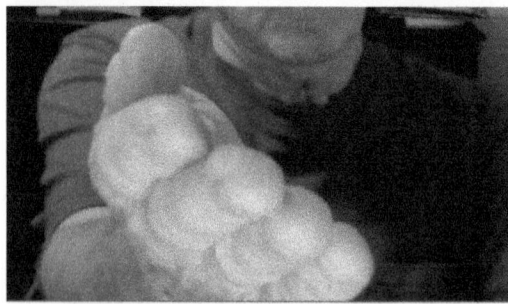

Initial entry movement

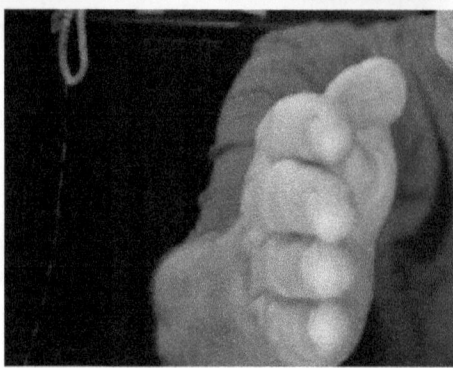

Entry: blade at blade depth

Chapter Five - Trunk Swing

> Trunk Swing
> It is a work of art. Divine is the feel. Ease and relaxation are paramount. There is a full range of movement, with hips projecting the Movement from Release to Entry. Sit lightly on the seat and let "the wind blow under your bottom". The shell slides easily beneath you.
>
> - Jimmy Joy

Trunk swing is either taught as the conventional approach with the abbreviated swing or the full swing movement. Abbreviated movement consists of setting the trunk angle out of the bow. In contrast, with the full trunk swing, the quantum approach, the body angle changes from the release to the entry with a steady movement from the hips. Fifty years ago, Fitzpatrick said that once you have experienced the swing, your body will never forget it; and he was right. To this day, with the first stroke, I can feel the integration at the entry, the solid connected drive, and the beauty of the release, followed by the simple glide and constant change in the trunk angle moving forward. The shell responds immediately, and I am carried back to those beautiful moments on the Henley course in St. Catharines, when I

Trunk Swing

first experienced the integration and flow of the stroke. I will never forget the feeling of exhilaration, power, and rhythm. I was experiencing the Flow State. My whole body was in a State of Flow with the shell. Everything felt so easy. This is really where the individual development of mind and consciousness occurs. George Pocock wrote, "I've heard men shriek with delight, when that swing came in an eight; it's a thing that they'll never forget as long as they live."

Trunk Swing is the foundation of the Stroke Cycle, the keystone in the arch of skill. He should really feel the movement of the hips forward and backward. It is the muscles of the hips that control the movement of the seat on the recovery. Steve Fairbairn wrote, "All races are won by the crew with the best forward swing." [29] In performing the stroke, the consistent positioning of the hands, arms, trunk legs and blade at the entry and the consistent positioning of the same at the release, is the basis for rhythm. The trunk swing serves the same purpose as a metronome. The extent of the stroke length is tight and uniform. So, it is safe to say that this is the most critical portion of the stroke cycle.

This hip movement is in phase with the run of the shell on the drive. There is Flow between the trunk and the shell. The trunk and legs complete the drive phase together followed by

---

[29] Steve Fairbairn, *Some Secrets of Successful Rowing*, p. 267

The Quantum Sculler

the arms. All three components begin together at the entry. This is an example of integral sculling with each of the three components connected. The trunk lays fifteen degrees beyond the perpendicular at the release. This is the ideal position to complete the power and to start forward for the next stroke in one movement. If he uses a longer layback, his release and initial recovery become a two-movement action. The incomparable Ned Hanlan likened the total action of the trunk swing to the pendular action of a clock. It is continuous action. It is Flow when coupled with the movement of the shell. The leg action should be steady, smooth and splayed shoulder-width during the swing forward, allowing enough room for the stomach. The stomach becomes distended as you move forward on the recovery and requires some space. Otherwise, it will press against the thighs shortening the stroke length. The sculler's body becomes part of Nature, part of the shell running under him. There is no separation between him and the external world of the seat and slide. It is an all-encompassing feeling and state of being. The specific details of the recovery require that the seat move a little when the trunk moves a little over the full course of the slide so that the body and seat arrive together at full reach. The knees end up perpendicular to the gunwales and splayed. The trunk is extended from the hips. On water the blade is carried to full extension. At full extension of the arms and trunk, the knuckles rise slightly followed by the pulling action and the raising of the wrists to execute the squaring action. The downward movement of the blade and the pulling action of the blade must be quick and done together. There is much less missing of water compared to having the blade prominently squared above the water, pause, then placed into the water in a deliberate but slow fashion. You have to feel the blade in your hands. At each end of the slide, the hands must be continually moving. This is an important ingredient for developing flow. Any large gap in these two movements is evident. Throughout the recovery, the trunk and legs are relaxed. It is in this part of the stroke that the sculler calms himself, eliminating any anxieties as he moves forward.

In sweep rowing, the trunk should be situated over the keel line for greater efficiency for most of the stroke. The linearity of the movement simply adds to the possibility of Flow being experienced by the athlete and the crew. Too often today, you find crews with wide handle holds and twisting the trunk towards the rigger at the entry. The arms become separated from the legs and the trunk, because they are not over the keel. These two components are not aligned. There is a loss of arm/trunk power that follows such positioning.

The Quantum Sculler

The Yale Lightweights over the keel at the release in 1970. Heads, elbows, arms, trunk, and legs are all in alignment.

The motion, when performed properly, becomes poetry of movement as the body flows forward and backward in a purposeful manner. It is all highly dependent on a cooperative and interdependent motion. The movements are solidly connected to a still mind, a mind that has been developed with countless hours of quiet sitting. This meditative state leads to freedom in the body movements.

The timing of the trunk action can be effectively covered in the winter months doing stroke simulation exercises without using the oar handle. It can take the form of part and whole

Trunk Swing

stroke drilling. After about three weeks, uniform movements develop in the group, exquisite timing that assists greatly to the balance of the shell once the crews go on the water. The drill can also be done on the water as a stationary exercise drill in the eight or four, with the athletes sitting at the backstops and swinging together, obtaining overall unity of movement. This drill really helps with their efficiency and group timing.

The primary drill for the recovery is part-slide rowing from 3/4, 1/2, 1/4, and full-slide from the back-end to full-slide front-end, using the oars, when on the water and without the oar handle, when on the ergometer indoors. The latter drills are referred to as simulation exercises. The simulation exercises are the "pump primers" for the athlete's imagination and for the visualization practices.

Eventually moving from the fall to the spring seasons, the trunk swing becomes an intimate part of the sculler. He accomplishes the swing with an intrinsic, unconscious movement. He simply does it without any thought to the actual process and Flow occurs.

Recovery – two seasonal approach approach:
a swing to a glide forward, fall to spring.

The Trunk Swing: a major key to flow.

The Five Movements of the release & follow through - hands, wrists, arms, trunk, legs - the sequence flows and appears as a single movement.

The fixed seat principle. Integrate the legs, trunk, arms at the entry as you would do on a fixed seat. At the end of the drive, trunk and legs finish together with arms trailing slightly.

←————————→ The distance the seat travels.

←——————————————→ The distance the shoulder (trunk) travels.

Timing = Trunk and Legs are synchronized with the blade work throughout the stroke cycle.

It takes a particular kind of coach to take this step-back and patiently work on the movements and the timing of the movements. He is an artist at work, a sculptor of the raw material in front of him. It is an intense and highly concentrated effort, both by the coach and the athlete. They are extremely committed to being exact.

Again, I am reminded of Teilhard de Chardin's important aphorism, "Seeing -You might say that the whole of life lies in that verb." [30] This timely advice from the great philosopher/scientist is extremely helpful as the crews are scrutinized over the next few weeks. Nothing goes un-checked. George Yeoman Pocock, felt, when you get the rhythm in an eight, it is

---

[30] Teilhard de Chardin, *The Phenomenon of Man*, p.31.

Trunk Swing

pure pleasure to be in it. It is not hard work when the rhythm comes – that "swing" as they call it.

Chapter Six - The Simulation Exercises

Simulation Exercises are pump primers for visualization. After a few weeks every body part is perfectly aligned. These drills are absolutely one of the best forms of training during the winter months. The timing of the bodies in the shell becomes impeccable.

- Jimmy Joy

The "swing" is developed in the winter months by daily simulation exercises. All the bodies become aligned and work in a tight highly uniformed fashion. After three weeks of this type of concentrated training, the crews look so uniform as every rower's shoulders, trunk, elbows and legs are perfectly aligned. The timing is exquisite. So, once the crews are able to get out on the water in the late spring they enjoy good balance in the shell because of these timing drills.

The photos of Lindsey Hochman [31] below show simulation exercises for the stages of the recovery, from zero to full slide without the handle. This is where the coach exercises his creativity in determining which section of the slide he wishes to

---

[31] Lindsey Hochman is now a coach at San Diego State University

The Simulation Exercises

stress for any particular training session. When done with a group of athletes, Entrainment occurs.[32] We also see it in synchronized swimmers' and dancers' routines. Examples of entrainment are all around us in Nature. We witness this entrainment with schools of fish and flocks of birds, especially the Canadian Geese.

These exercises were used successfully during my tenure at MIT, Yale, Wesleyan, and with Hobart; done in the tanks at Yale, and on the ergometers at the other three locations. These drills were done usually without the handle as a daily part of practice. It was an opportunity to be very intensive with coaching, both on an individual and group basis. The athlete has a great opportunity to feel the Movements as he performs the parts of the stroke in slow motion. It is a process of refinement and careful attention to the details of the Movements and the posture of the body. It is this attention to detail in this part of the stroke cycle by athlete and coach that leads directly to the achievement of Flow. I recall how in the first four months of learning the Fitzpatrick stroke, I had to think about this process of the trunk to seat movement. However, in the next four

---

[32] Entrainment is a process in which one rhythmic frequency influences another, until they synchronize, or approach synchronization, or have a strong influence on each other - much as waves of water influence one another when they intersect.

months the movement became intrinsic and I moved with the shell in a preliminary flow state.

These are extremely high concentration exercises as the athlete focuses on each of the movements of the stroke cycle. He is looking for balance in his body, alignment, and relaxation. Doing the exercises with this type of concentration, drills become almost meditative. The drill focuses on the uniformity of the body action, arms, elbows, trunk, knees, and legs throughout the stroke cycle. It is truly amazing what can be accomplished doing these drills over the winter months on a regular basis.

Below is Lindsey Hochman at various points in the recovery from the Release to Entry positions. Note the change in the trunk angle from the Release to the Entry.

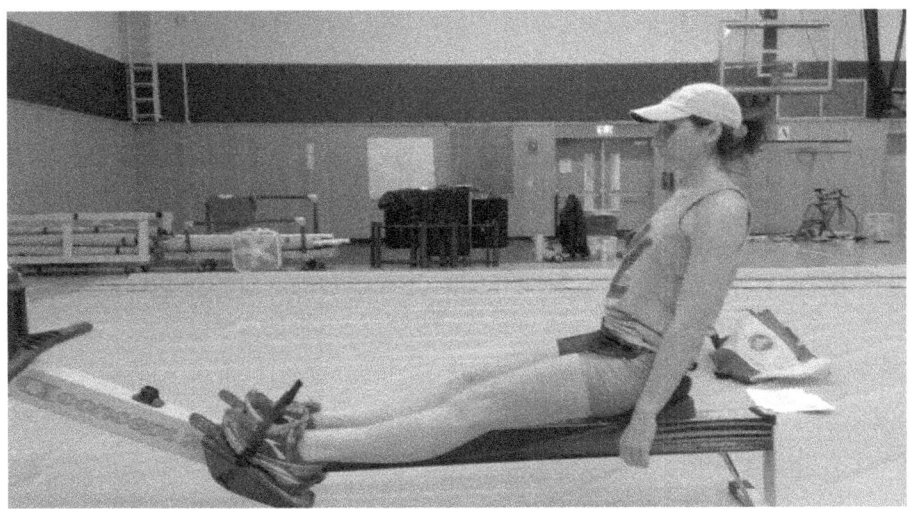

Back end slide

The Simulation Exercises

Back End of the Slide without the Handle

Back-end Slide without the Handle

The Simulation Exercises

Three-quarters slide without the handle.

Note: The angle of the legs at this point on the slide is about 60 degrees. This critical positioning is more fully described in Chapter Four. The front edge of the seat is not too close to the heels. This should also be the position of the legs at full-slide. The coach in one of his many roles, in this case the choreographer, should monitor this item closely with each member of the crew.

Full-slide without the handle

Note: The front edge of the seat is a little too close to the heels here. Again, the role of choreographer for the coach comes into play with such important details.

.

Chapter Seven - Beyond Materialism

"This spiritual crisis occurs when people find themselves trapped in an outmoded, suffocating network of values and conceptions, in an ineffective worldview, a creed outworn, that has become too small to allow the people to get on with their cultural evolution." [33]

- Michael N. Nagler

We have a spiritual crisis in our society at large and a special crisis in our sport practice. Our focus is much too narrow and centered on ourselves and our thoughts on programming and training. We should enlarge our cultural awareness beyond the narrow confines of ourselves and rowing. We have to read more deeply and engage in the practice of experiencing periodic silence. Our inner self is barren and as Pythagoras said, "learn to be silent. Let your quiet mind listen and absorb the silence." We must be committed to trying new approaches before we fully understand them. Awareness must include our life both in and

---

[33] Michael N. Nagler, *Our Spiritual Crisis: Recovering Human Wisdom in a Time of Violence*

out of the shell. We must read broadly and try to set aside a few minutes each day to meditate, reflect, and ponder.

Krishnamurti agrees: "This quietness, this silence is the highest form of intelligence which is never personal, never yours or mine. Being anonymous, it is whole and immaculate." We must recognize that "interconnectivity is not only the law of physics and of nature, but also forms the basis of community and compassion- compassion is the working out of our shared interconnectivity." [34] As the late physicist David Bohm stated, "I propose a post-modern physics which begins with the whole. "We have to consider in developing the training program the whole person - the mind, the body, and the spirit.

According to Llewellyn Vaughan-Lee, "the feminine knows this oneness. She feels it in her body, in her instinctual wisdom. She knows its interconnectedness. Now it is time for this wisdom of the feminine to be combined with masculine consciousness, so that anew understanding of the wholeness of life can be used to help us to heal the world." [35] All coaches, both masculine and feminine, have to discover and practice this feminine side in their coaching. This is the wholistic approach, the "soft" approach. Vaughan-Lee feels that, "by combing the masculine and feminine wisdom we can come to understand the re-

---

[34] Matthew Fox, *The Pope's War*, p.235
[35] Llewellyn Vaughan-Lee, *Reclaiming the Feminine Mystery of Creation*, Parabola Spring 2016, p.23

lationships between the parts and the whole, and if we listen we can hear life telling us how to redress this imbalance." [36] It is a deep thinker quiet type of leadership that we are advocating.

George Pocock, a philosopher/poet, a quantum sculler, a master boat builder, and an excellent resource coach for Olympic crews from 1924 to 1964, is an excellent example of the quiet leadership that we advocate for rowing athletes. George had a fine eye for technique and for the mental qualities in the athletes that he touched. He was a master artist in every sense of the word.

Harry Parker, the coach of Harvard crews for over fifty years, displayed this same type of quiet leadership for his students. He was not only physically fit, but deeply cerebral. He thought and reflected deeply on what he was doing with his athletes. He combined the power of the mind with the body, and with the power of the spirit. Through his lengthy periods of silence, he was at the same time giving himself space to assess the situation at hand and giving his athletes space to figure things out and to perform. Harry was the consummate coach. He forged the beautiful union of the physiological with the movement training, and the psychological. He was admired, respect-

---

[36] Llewellyn Vaughan-Lee, *Reclaiming the Feminine Mystery of Creation*, Parabola, Spring 2016, p.23

ed, and loved by his athletes. Harry remains the outstanding model of the integral coach over the past fifty years.

Llewellyn Vaughan-Lee feels, "that the feminine can give us an understanding of how all the diverse parts of life relate together, their patterns of relationship, the interconnections that nourish life. She can help us to see consciously what she knows instinctively, that all is part of a living, organic whole, in which all of the parts of creation communicate together, and that each cell of creation expresses the whole a unique way." [37] We must, as coaches, employ open-mindedness, strong skills of empathy and caring, as well as the patience to take time to meditate and to listen to our athletes. We need the courage to try the novel in our coaching, if we are to achieve some measure of the feminine in that pursuit. The feminine is focused on our inner world while the masculine concentrates on the outer world and that which is measurable. We need both aspects. Vaughan-Lee goes on, "An understanding of the organic wholeness of life belongs to the instinctual knowing of the feminine, but combined with masculine consciousness this can be communicated in words, not just feelings. We can combine the science of the mind and the senses with the inner knowing. We can give a blueprint of

---

[37] Llewellyn Vaughan-Lee, *Reclaiming the Feminine Mystery of Creation*, Parabola, Spring 2016, p.26

the planet that will enable us to live in creative harmony with all of life." [38]

Wendell Berry in his new book, *Our Only World*, writes, "We need to acknowledge the formlessness inherent in analytic science that divides creatures into organs, cells, and ever smaller parts or particles according to its technological capacities.

I recognize the possibility and existence of this knowledge, even its usefulness, but I also recognize the narrowness of its usefulness and the damage it does. I can see that in a sense it is true, but also that its truth is small and far from complete.

In and by all my thoughts and acts, I am opposed to any claim that such knowledge is adequate to the sustenance of human life or the health of the ecosphere." [39]

On a smaller scale, we have the same thing happening in sport, where we display so much reliance on the material side of things. We, as coaches, seem to be programmed by the ergometer and a myriad of other test results. The result is that the statistical logs on our athletes are bulging. However, how much attention is given to the quality of each movement that the athlete makes during a practice session? Huston Smith, a well-known author and religious studies scholar, has labeled this, *Scientism*, "the belief that the facts available to normal science are the only

---
[38] Llewellyn Vaughan-Lee, *Reclaiming the Feminine Mystery of Creation*, Parabola, Spring 2016, p.26
[39] Wendell Berry, *Our Only World*

reality." Or, this view of Scientism from neuroscientist and philosopher Raymond Tallis, "that it is the mistaken belief that the natural sciences (physics, biology, chemistry and their derivatives) can or will give a complete description and even explanation of everything, including human life."[40] Specifically, in coaching, we continue with only the numbers in mind. We are too much localized and there is not enough of the whole in our coaching methods. Recently, attending a college crew practice, the coach in charge never once said anything to his athletes about their technique. His only concern was with numbers that they were programmed to achieve. It is critical that we communicate to the athletes how they are performing, rather than let these obvious flaws go unnoticed and uncorrected. This shift in emphasis in the training from technique to solely the physical training today occurred in the 1970s.

This is particularly pervasive in the American sporting world and it is the case in the present coaching practices of rowing and sculling. The ergometer score rules, along with the "stroke coach". Today, we are too reductionist in our pursuit of metrics. Numbers from the amount of weight lifted, in erg scores and speed of the shell over short distances. We

---

[40] Raymond Tallis, *Aping Mankind: Neuromania, Darwinitis and the Misrepresentation of Humanity*, p.15

cannot see, for example, that the ergometer can be used for something other than tests and physical training.

In correspondence from January 2016, Nich Lee Parker, coach of Columbia lightweights, wrote, "I have been encountering this same preoccupation with numbers more and more. I find that the "better" recruits are coming from places where they use a lot of technology and math to determine selection and put a quantitative association with technical changes. It takes some explaining to convince them that the math going into these numbers is so reduced, that it isn't very reliable for the whole picture. Our upperclassmen have learned this through experience and are continuing to develop an awareness of things around them and finding that in that they are able to make improvements to the run of the hull. Mindfulness is the most important thing that is separating what we are doing from anyone else. I think that there is a larger discussion that needs to be had about how, when, and if one should include technology in coaching. The more I study, the more I see how limited that information is, when compared to what the "quantum sculler" will be able to absorb regarding making the boat run smoothly and effectively." [41]

The coach simply does not address any concern or emphasis on the movement development of the athlete. I am speak-

---

[41] Correspondence from Nich Lee Parker on 29 January 2016

ing of the need for a heightened state of awareness from athlete and coach. However, with this latter approach, significant progress can be reached with both the athlete's skills and the development of the coach's eye. With this heightened attention and purpose on making smoother movements comes enjoyment, pure joy in feeling the fluidity of the motion. Athletes and coaches, fully enjoy the accomplishment. Both learn and experience.

Physicist Max Planck, at the beginning of the quantum revolution, stated the following, "Consciousness, I regard as fundamental. I regard matter as derivative from consciousness ... everything that we regard as existing postulates consciousness." This is a very prophetic statement, yet still inaccessible to the public, because of the influence of present-day media. We must shift from a system of thought premised on an order of matter to energy to consciousness to the inverse of consciousness to energy to matter, CEM. This shift in consciousness will permit us to break out of this dismal materialism. For the sculling coach, this means that coaching of movement training will be emphasized and consciousness development becomes more of a priority.

It was Frank Dick, former director of coaching for British Athletics, who said, "Attempting to increase a speed of execution without maintaining technical quality is, however, disastrous. Introducing speed without fracturing the integrity of the technical skill is achievable given carefully judged increments of stimuli to do so." [42] The coach must be extremely careful that any increase in speed training is not done at the expense of good movements that should be consolidated in the athletes' motions. With this coaching approach he much more attuned to the wholeness in his method. He is considering more than one factor.

I feel it begins with our main objective in sport training, our concern for the personal development of the athlete, and the establishment of smooth movements in the overall stroke cycle. With this in mind, at all levels, we should engage in whole stroke coaching. Coaching of the parts is a return to Newtonian physics. We must realize that everything in the stroke and in our lives is connected. We must become more aware and comfortable with the quantum world. It is the sculler's educational development that is critical for his progress and not the simple materialistic goal of winning. With this humanistic approach, the coach has a significant influence on the development of the athlete's beautiful mind. In the Ghandi Model, the individual serves the family, the family serves the community, the community serves the nation, and the nation serves the world. He referred to this as the "oceanic circle." The coach should be aware of this model.

---

[42] Frank Dick, *Winning Matters*, p.188

The Quantum Sculler

    For interior development, it is important that each individual includes meditative practice as part of his training. Some seventy-five colleges and universities in the United States now have programs of some kind in contemplative practices. So there is some effort being initiated in these institutions moving toward developing a mode of knowing, that is above the intellect. But, we cannot wait until your institution offers a few courses on Contemplative Practices. You have to introduce regular practice of the different modes. These include quiet sitting, relaxation, visualization, concentration, and mindfulness training. This modality should be an integral dimension of your overall training plan. With quiet sitting, we must monitor the posture of the actual sitting position, as any slouching will carry over into the shell. From this good sitting position we can then introduce the concepts of stillness, solitude, simplicity, and silence that we are seeking in the mind.

    British tennis player Johanna Konta, in January 2016, vaulted from a 148 ranking to number 48 in the world. She attributes her ascent to an overhaul of her mental state, rather than her game. She is a recovering achiever, having shifted her focus from the outcome to the process. She emphasizes "staying in the moment" and "really finding my enjoyment within the sport, really separating that enjoyment from results." Konta expanded on that thought. "I think if you live and die with your wins and losses, it is an incredibly tough lifestyle to live," she said. "So I think really separating myself from that gave me a lot of enjoyment and perspective." She ended up being eliminated in the semi-finals, her highest achievement to date. But, her approach to the competition is noteworthy. She is engaged in a soft, wholistic, and humanistic process.

Meister Eckart, the wonderful thirteenth century Dominican monk, stated, "Most of us think too much about what we should do and not enough about what we should be. If we would pay more attention to what we should be, our work would shine forth bright." [43] This is where our attention remains in the moment, in the now, improving our consciousness. This is the mindset for skill development and the improvement of our inner consciousness. The process of interior development starts with slowing down and paying attention to the mind doing one thing at a time with complete concentration." You rest quietly on the present moment." [44] To confront our concerns and our anxieties, as well as to meet the stress of competition and in some cases championship play, we have at our disposal the benefits of daily deep, and quiet repose. We slow down, repeat our selected mantram and engage in one pointed attention - the act of mindfulness and living in the now.

---

[43] Eknath Easwaran, *Strength in the Storm: Transforming Stress, Live in Balance and Find Peace of Mind*, p.56.

[44] Eknath Easwaran, *Strength in the Storm: Transforming Stress, Live in Balance and Find Peace of Mind*, p.61

The Quantum Sculler

This spiritual development moves beyond our sensitivity to self, to include others, non-human creations and to God who is situated within and beyond this totality. This obviously includes the "inter-being" of all, sentient existence. By inter-being we recognize that we are connected to every living and nonliving thing in the universe.

An example of concern for the non-human occurred in the 1928 Olympics. Bob Pearce had easily advanced in the first two rounds of competition in single sculls of the Summer Games in Amsterdam before an odd occurrence in the quarterfinals allowed Pearce to show that he was truly a nice guy. While competing against a French opponent, a family of ducks passed in front of Pearce in the middle of his lane. Pearce actually just sat there and let the ducks pass. Once they were completely clear, he took off and still easily won his race. Then he went on to win the Gold Medal in the competition and set a record for the event that stood until Petti Karppinen set a new record 48 years later in the 1976 Olympics. He also went on to win the Gold Medal in the competition.

A comment by Philosopher and Mathematical Physicist Henry Stapp is helpful, "The assimilation of this quantum conception of man into the cultural environment of the twenty-first century must inevitably produce a shift in values conducive to human survival. The quantum conception gives an enlarged

Beyond Materialism

sense of self from which must flow lofty values that extend far beyond the confines of narrow personal self-interest." [45]

Yes, the quantum mental approach takes us well beyond our immediate concern for our sport practice. We begin to observe the world around us with totally different eyes. We cannot be dictated by the narrow choice of just winning in sport. We have to work on a more cooperative, expansive mind and a concentrated movement training approach. These are the lofty values to which Stapp is referring. He would argue that we must attempt to achieve Flow, in the shell, as well as out of the shell for the rest of our life. Thus, we are working on our spiritual selves.

---

[45] H. Stapp, *Quantum Physics and Human Values*, a paper, p.8-9

Chapter Eight - Training the Spirit

There is neither spirit nor matter in the world; the stuff of the universe is spirit - matter. No other substance, but this, could produce the human molecule.
    - Teilhard de Chardin

Training the spirit is the bedrock of any training program designed to fully develop the athlete. Spirit Training is probably the most neglected aspect of the three-pronged approach of the physical, mental, and spiritual aspects of training. These three dimensions comprise the integral coaching approach. All three must be programmed and executed on a daily basis, especially with the very nature of the sport as it is practiced outdoors for most of the year. So there can be a fine connection nurtured with the natural world. This nurturing process must start in early childhood before they come to rowing. Get them away from the computer and the video games. However, it is critical that their athletes relate to the outer natural world. This is the method by which their inner world will flourish if stimulated by the wonders of nature. Our natures flourish from the inside out. Thus, there must be time set aside for the crew or sculler to meditate and meditate deeply. Similar to molding of the body, molding of the mind, must also be practiced on a daily basis.

Thomas Berry has said, "What has been forgotten is the inner life of humans and the outer life of the natural world." [46] This deep spirituality has its roots in this bond between the human and the natural worlds, "the inner and outer landscapes are connected." It now seems to be a lost element in our evolution. However, as we come ever closer in our relationship to nature, we increase our sense of the Spiritual. For the athlete, this commences with his daily practice of quiet sitting both on land and in the shell. While seated in the shell, he must start each practice with a quick observation of the environment around him beginning with his position in the shell and move outward to take in the natural world around him.

You, as a coach, raise your own consciousness level through your reading, study, and meditative experiences both in and out of the shell. The athlete can follow your example. So, his spirit is elevated by his daily quiet sitting and by his daily observance of the natural world around him. His inner and outer growth will directly be reflected in his physical performance and in his personality. George Pocock would ask, "Where is the spir-

---

[46] Carolyn W. Toben, *Recovering a Sense of the sacred: Conservations with Thomas Berry*, p.37

itual value of rowing? The losing of self entirely to the cooperative effort of the crew as a whole." [47]

The wonderful geotheologian Thomas Berry adds, "Quantum physics tell us that every atom influences every other atom without a known signal passing through the intervening space. I like to say we are not ourselves without everything and everyone else. [48] Berry employed the term communion, which is meant to understand the inter-relationship of the universe within itself and the interconnectedness of each part with the whole - the interior binding force of the universe. [49] This philosophy would be expressed fully beyond the United Nations to a United Species as the comprehensive state that which we all belong. [50] Pocock did not envisage his philosophy achieving this proportion of influence, but it is certainly a goal for rowing and sport in general.

I am reminded of the words of Wendell Berry expressing his love of knowledge of the land. The sculling coach can employ these same sentiments: "I have, from my own experience begun to know, how intimately related, how nearly synonymous are the terms 'love' and 'know', how likely impossible it is to know

---

[47] Daniel James Brown, *The Boys in the Boat*, p.353.
[48] Carolyn W. Toben, *Recovering a Sense of the Sacred: Conversations with Thomas Berry*, p.59.
[49] Carolyn W. Toben, *Recovering a Sense of the Sacred: Conversations with Thomas Berry*, p.59
[50] Brian Swimme & Thomas Berry, *The Universe Story*, p.4.

authentically or well what one does not love, and how certainly impossible it is to love what one does not know." [51]

Berry is speaking about the husbandry of his land as a small Kentuckian working farmer, in the face of industrial farming and their preoccupation with statistics and mechanization. There are lessons to be learned here for our sculling. This in large part is where we derive and foster our spirit with our connection to the natural world.

Over the years, both as an athlete and coach, I have felt this strong inner feeling, and the resulting inner and outer enthusiasm to aspire to a higher consciousness level. This inner form is not separate reality from the world around us. We must evolve our democracy to a "biocracy" to include the lives of the larger earth community. But never did I connect this spiritual development to an interationship with the Divine and to the earth that Berry references. Pocock confines his thoughts solely to the Divine. However, it is imperative that we recover "our intuitive awareness of the natural world, this interior, inner soul dimension that has been lost." We have become too secular with the exception of the indigenous peoples throughout the world. Our daily sculling should include this larger perspective of our spiritual development.

---

[51] Wendell Berry, *Our Only World*, p. 116

> It's a great art, is rowing.
> It's the finest art there is.
> It's a symphony of motion.
> And when you're rowing well,
> Why it's nearing perfection.
> And when you reach perfection
> You're touching the Divine.
> It touches the you of yous,
> Which is your soul. [52]
>
> - George Yeoman Pocock

Eco-philosopher and scientist Thomas Berry has said, "What has been forgotten is the inner life of humans and the outer life of the natural world." [53] This deep spirituality has its roots in this bond between the human and the natural worlds, "the inner and outer landscapes are connected." It now seems to be a lost element in our evolution. However, as we come ever closer in our relationship to nature, we increase our sense of the Spiritual. However, it is important and critical that we relate to the good earth. This becomes the major source of a deep spirituality. Thomas Berry writes, "The earth is origin, our nourish-

---

[52] Gordon Newell, *Ready All! George Yeoman Pocock and Crew Racing*, p.2.
[53] Carolyn W. Toben, *Recovering a Sense of the sacred: Conservations with Thomas Berry*, p.37

ment, our educator our healer, our fulfillment. At its core, even our spirituality is Earth derived." [54] We must try to push beyond the world of human artifice, and find our deeper spirituality in the natural world. As I write this passage, I quickly glance and admire the ten trees dotting our backyard and the small wild wooded area beyond. I take this in each day as a reminder of my spiritual being.

For the athlete, this commences with his daily practice of quiet sitting both on land and in the shell. While seated in the shell, he must start each practice with a quick observation of the environment around him beginning with his position in the shell and move outward to take in the natural world around him.

I recall watching USA Olympian Brad Lewis, a National Coach, stop his crew in the middle of a training run three days before the World Championship, so that they could observe the beauty of the sunset. He was ensuring that his athletes were connected to the natural world. It was a wonderful moment by set up a good coach. In contrast, at the other end of the basin, I found a coach berating his athlete, who was reduced to tears and to an eventual sub-par performance in the Championships.

We slow down, quieting the mind, experiencing the profound silence of our existence, thinking intuitively and then we move our total being to a profound level of spirituality. Play,

---

[54] Thomas Berry, *The Sacred Universe*, p. 69

humor, and frivolity are all important elements in this process of developing wholeness. The furrowed brow has nothing do with lifting the weight. We can't be so overly concerned with improvement, that we overlook enjoying the moment, the run of the shell, the long practice, the beauty of the river, the sunset and sunrise, the race, the lifting of the weight, and all of the ancillary activities that are associated with the sport.

The one exercise besides rowing that seems to help re-establish some degree of healthy and restful mental framework for these young athletes is meditation. With this daily practice, stress and anxiety levels were greatly reduced and the central focus on rowing practice is established. The organism had been reset for optimal practice performance. The coach must sit with his athletes daily and this becomes the basis for communication and mutual respect. So, quiet sitting is programmed into some part of training. It is the initial vehicle for entrance into the profound world of the spirit from an over-stimulated world. Experiencing silence and solitude has a direct impact on the progress of athletic experience. Further to this practice, is the repeating of a mantram. Gandhi used *Rama, Rama, Rama*, that is calling on the source of joy in our hearts. In the Eastern Orthodox traditions, *Lord, Jesus Christ, have mercy on us*, is used, Buddhist mantras *Om mani padme hum*, Muslims repeat *Allah*, the Jews use *Blessed art thou, O Lord* and a non-denominational Mantra could simply be *Peace, Peace, Peace*. The use of a mantram addresses the one pointed attention practice and goes a long way to reduce our fears and anxieties. It is an excellent way to achieve one posted attention and to cope with the stress of the moment. It provides the space necessary to handle a stressful situation. The total meditative sequence includes introducing quiet sitting and mindful breathing, along with the body scan. These practices are followed with relaxation, visualization and concentration practice. Quiet Sitting transforms into slow motion on the ergometer on land and in the shell on the water. The slow motion silent rows with closed eyes are extremely productive; developing stillness, as well as non-judgment and open-hearted moment-to-moment thinking. The objective is the "Beginner's Mind."

Relaxation can be introduced early in the fall during water practices. Our consciousness grows as we become more skilled. This occurs as the sculling becomes finer and finer. We learn to heighten our ability to relax the body and the finer parts of movements through our finger actions. Relaxation and enjoyment really are the foundation for racing. We simply enjoy the sport and the training. With the relaxed state, we are less anxious and are capable of increased power production. Relaxation practice of the body before competition reduces anxiety levels, increases the magnitude of consciousness and skill advancement, frees up the production of more powerful movements, and allows the spiritual body to flourish. Beyond stillness, it furnishes silence, solitude, and simplicity, the four important "s" words. As such, it is an excellent recipe for race preparation and delivery. It should not be overlooked in getting the athlete ready for competition. With this type of preparation, the athlete proceeds into competition with a lighter and more focused integrated body.

Visualization skills are enhanced indoors during the winter months with stroke simulation exercises, with or without holding the handle on the ergometer. These practices performed on a daily basis throughout the training year develop a shift in your inner presence to a more serene, yet alert, inner self - you feel it. Stabilization practice occurs when you are able to concentrate for longer periods, especially by doing stroke simulation exercises without the handle on the ergometer.

For the athlete, quiet sitting requires good posture and good breathing. Sitting can be done both indoors and outdoors when the weather is milder. It is important for me to sit from time to time amongst the trees or in the back garden. This type of activity brings you closer to the natural world, wherein lies your ultimate strength.

In our sculling, we begin with the relationship to our inner being and then relate our inner selves to our immediate external environment, our physical bodies, and particularly to our posture in the shell. Finally, you begin to observe and relate to the natural world of our practice location with its animals and birds, its trees and bank shrubbery that serves as a perimeter for our practice.

So there are four elements to consider: inner nature, external bodies, external equipment, and relationship to the natural world of animals, birds, trees and foliage. These four elements represent the merging of "the inner life of the human with the outer life of the natural world."

For a few of us, modern development has not encased our waterways. Our canal in the Finger Lakes is a beautiful, pristine setting. But, for the large majority of practitioners, they must contend with buildings lining the banks. In some cases, it becomes a difficult search to find a tree, or bush, or a bit of grass. For me, I am fortunate, for I begin each day by looking at the many trees found in our backyard. It is easy to feel the bark and smell the foliage. It is wonderful therapy, a constant delight, and a timely reminder to fully engage the natural world each day.

However, it is important and critical that we relate to the good earth. This becomes the major source of a deep spirituality. Eco-philosopher and scientist Thomas Berry writes, "The earth is origin, our nourishment, our educator our healer, our fulfillment. At its core, even our spirituality is Earth derived." [55] We must try to push beyond the world of human artifice, and find

---

[55] Thomas Berry, *The Sacred Universe*, p. 69

our deeper spirituality in the natural world. As I write this passage, I quickly glance and admire the ten trees dotting our backyard and the small wild wooded area beyond. I take this in each day as a reminder of my spiritual being.

We must keep in mind that this is an evolutionary process; moving the viewer to greater complexity and higher consciousness before our very eyes. Our skills should change and become finer and finer movements. This is complex and it requires a higher level of consciousness. This is especially true in our use of the fingers on the handle, as we advance in our skill, using less and less of our palms and rely more and more on relaxed fingers. We begin to focus purely on our minds, as we are pulling light and relaxed. This is never more the case than in the finger action. Fingers must be relaxed as they extend further outward at the entry. We see this in the positioning of Ernest James Barry's hands. It is an unusual action and sensation this "mind pulling." Everything feels light and there is little focus on the rest of the body parts. It is effortless. It is a totally whole movement.

We must be alert and concentrated for these changes to occur on a regular basis. Matter and spirit come together in a sensitive communion of deep cooperation. We are probing the depths of own stillness and subjectivity. By doing so, we come to realize the world around us is one of subjects, rather than objects. George Pocock realized this truth when he wrote, "A good shell has to have a life and resiliency to get in harmony with the swing of the crew." The crew, the nine bodies and the shell were one. They forge one very large spirit.

With the relationship between athlete and coach, there must be trust, respect, freedom, awareness, listening, and a deep appreciation of each other. We, athlete and coach, must be committed to an awareness, education, and search for transcendence in our consciousness, every day, relative to the three areas of physical, mental, and spiritual training. Every training session should involve some element of each component. When this is accomplished, we have integral training working. To accomplish this heightened degree of focused attention, there must be a balance between levity, serious play, as well as self-directed and coach-directed skill training. These practices have a direct effect on the attitude of the athlete.

It is important that in emphasizing our external body that we concentrate on the smooth and continuous movement of the body. From there we go to the sculls and to the blade work with fingers and hands seen as being the blades. Each end of the slide involves a continuous movement of the blade into and out of the water. These are effortless movements. Then it falls to the run of the shell and our position over the keel line to make the flow of the shell a fluid simple drive action of the body and the legs. In the sweep, it means using a narrow grip and a slightly bent inside arm to keep you over the keel line. With the wide handhold, there occurs a separation of these critical elements of the trunk and legs action that leads to fragmentation in the drive action.

In my own coaching career, I became extremely sensitive to the pain, personal issues, and "baggage" that the athletes on the team were carrying. Promoting empathy within the group is extremely beneficial for everyone. This deep empathy is yet another primary quality for developing the spirit in the self and in the team. A modern psychologist, Ken Wilber, feels, "that the capacity to take the role of others, to see perspectives different from our own, to put ourselves in others' shoes - these are all the ways that consciousness stretches and grows." [56] This is the development of empathy. Promoting empathy within the group is extremely beneficial for everyone and it fosters group spirit.

Deep empathy is yet another primary quality for developing spirit in the self, in the team, and in the body. A team, a community, and the world, work most effectively when the parts are functioning interdependently and holistically. Thomas Berry refers to this as the "quality of communion", where we realize that everything and everyone are connected. The whole organism needs to embrace the body, the mind and the spirit. A program of training for the spirit completes the true integral coaching method. This component requires the most attention

---

[56] Ken Wilber, *What is Enlightenment?* p.110

by today's coaching community. The young athlete today has so much external stimuli that did not confront young athletes fifty years ago. When you reach beyond your self, you are committing to a different type of lifestyle. You are committing yourself to the silence of the inner self.

With this integral coaching method, empathy becomes the main root for the development of individual and group spirit. Empathy displayed by the coach serves as a standard operating model for everyone associated with the team. Teammates develop caring and understanding for each other. It creates an air of cooperation that is so vital in the development of the team. As we know, it is in our individual bodies, a biological fact.

Our power resides in silence. I vividly recall, in the early Canadian spring, in the moments in my early youth, of sitting quietly with my dog Skippy beside the swimming hole on 12 Mile Creek. I was enjoying the morning sun, and gazing at the beautiful bank of white Trilliums on the escarpment in front of me. It was the perfect place and opportunity for quiet reflection. I came away from these moments exhilarated and refreshed. This weekly activity would be my initial memory of my relating to the beauty and wonder of nature. This Sunday morning ritual was my early beginning with meditation moments. I was 10 years old at the time and parents today would not allow a child to take a six-mile hike into the woods under his own surveillance. In addition, I recall never tiring of our family trips to Niagara Falls and witnessing the absolute power of the water dropping over 100 feet.

The athlete's spirit is expressed in his power of focus and his mindfulness of the immediate environment and the task at hand. Total awareness on the part of the athlete, no matter what he is doing, becomes part of his deeper being, his spirit. We have to be open in mind and heart and must let go of negative situations.

Of course we need to ask, how do we further train the spiritual? My study and experience have identified the following as the means to enhance the individual and group spirit -- emphasizing the wholeness of things, embracing Nature, developing empathy, seeking challenges, engaging in play, embracing reflection, and being mindful on a daily basis. Again, the importance of mindfulness in the process of spirituality is stressed. This is the direction that in the 21st century we need to follow, according to Thomas Berry, and it is also an ambitious plan for coaches, and our athletes. It is much more critical than simply planning for winning. We have been given a competitive instinct, not to compete with others but to compete with ourselves.[57] This is a major adjustment to our mental framework.

---

[57] Eknath Easwaran, *Strength in the Storm: Transform Stress , Live in Balance, and Find Peace of Mind*, p.129.

Training the Spirit

It certainly conveys a great deal of our planning and goal setting efforts.

These are avenues for fostering growth of this important element, not only in our athletic experience, but generally in life. Great leaders and great people have this quality as part of their central core of being. This characteristic is behind their unshakeable drive to carry out their life's mission. The athlete's disposition, attitude, or spirit should remain a constant throughout the highs and lows of training. It is an unshakeable dimension of our inner self. Man is ultimately a spirit. "Spirit is the summit of being, the highest rung on the ladder of evolution and the wood out of which the entire ladder and all its rungs are made" [58] Therefore, Spirit is both transcendent and immanent. This analogy can be applied to the ideal athlete. The coach recognizes that the athlete should be mentally present, which is immanence, and operating with the highest level of concentrated intensity, which is transcendence. We begin with immanence and mindfulness. The coach wants the athlete focused in the present, and on the task. He wants the athlete to be fully and enthusiastically engaged with whatever activity is confronting him - Mindfulness.

We slow down, quieting the mind, experiencing the profound silence of our existence, thinking intuitively. Then we

---

[58] Ken Wilber, *The Essential Ken Wilber*, p.51

move our total being to a profound level of spirituality. Play, humor, and frivolity are all important elements in this process of developing wholeness. The furrowed brow has nothing do with lifting the weight. We cannot be so overly concerned with improvement, that we overlook enjoying the moment, the run of the shell, the long practice, the beauty of the river, the sunset and sunrise, the race, the lifting of the weight, and all of the ancillary activities that are associated with the sport.

The "academic" coach, the statistics-driven coach, assumes that consciousness is not important, and that our unconscious mind cannot be trusted; only that which can be measured is of value and everything must be objective and scientific. His research and study only includes the superficial dimension. He completely overlooks and discounts the inward approach to coaching. He is one-dimensional. His approach is to use the upper mind only. It is rational and is slower-working than the lower mind. The lower mind is more intuitive, nimble, involuntary and automatic. It is quicker and more fluid. However, this type of coach has no room for the intrinsic or the intuitive approach. I suggest that we require both for effective programming. Both modes of thought involve the larger reality of life.

Mindfulness is a key element in the training of the sculler. The athlete trains to remain in the moment exercising strong attention skills. These mindfulness skills are honed and refined both during the land and on-water training. On land, an effec-

Training the Spirit

tive mindfulness exercise is the body scan. Scanning involves feeling the state of each part of the body without judgment. The scan makes you aware of the state of each part of your body, whether it is relaxed, or tense, or in a neutral state. Other exercises to foster this quality are slow motion rowing on the erg and part-stroke drills for the recovery. Here you try to feel the body pivoting from the hips up the full length of the slide. The mindfulness is actually unconsciously developed through the practice of these meditative practices. Mindfulness training enlarges our spirit, our attention, and concentration. It allows the athlete to fully utilize the benefits of both mental and physical training. With regular practice, our physical selves and our consciousness undergo great evolutionary development as athlete and coach, both becoming more animated and closer to their animal selves. You are opening up the sensitivities of your porous skin and your spinal cord to the offerings of Nature around you. In this opening-up you begin to realize that you are Nature. You have all the qualities of a skilled woodsman, like "Natty" Bumppo, the protagonist of James Fenimore Cooper's pentalogy of frontier novels known as the Leatherstocking Tales.

Robin Wall Klimmerer earned a PhD in Botany and is a member of the Citizen Potawatomi Nation, a Native American people originally from the Great Lakes, with a reservation today, in Oklahoma. She describes herself as a traveller between the scientific and indigenous ways of knowing. She seems to be standing still, looking simultaneously through two lenses, expressing two world views. Trees for her, are photosynthesizing beings as well as teachers. A forest is an ecosystem and a home at once.[59] By familiarizing ourselves with Robin Wall Kimmerer's writings and viewpoints, we broaden our perspective and go much beyond the western scientific view of life. We begin to relate to trees, our plant and animal life, all of which are incorporated into our home on the waterways. It becomes another critical dimension of our involvement with rowing, for us as well as our athletes. We too have a second mind. We begin to see that we cannot evaluate the athlete in isolation from his peers. Thus, we recognize that certain persons, in combination with others, make shells move, in spite of their individual numbers from the ergometer or the amount of weight lifted. Such a perspective involves visualizing the total person -- the mental, physical, and spiritual athlete.

Training of the spirit involves specific programming for a level of consciousness that reaches beyond the Centaur state.[60] It is simply a refinement and increased sensitivity of quiet sitting, visualization, relaxation, concentration, and Mindfulness Practices. When this occurs, movement becomes flow and the

---

[59] Leah Tonino, Robin Wall Kimmerer, *On Scientific and Native American Views of the Natural World*, April 2016, The Sun

[60] This Centaur level is the third level in Ken Wilber's model of consciousness development.

organism is fully integrated with the environment. In the shell, Mindfulness can be accomplished by two drills -- slow motion rowing that develops our attention levels and quarter-slide quick rowing at higher rates. It is living in the now with a realization that everything is connected. It is pure Quantum living. Our sensitivity to wholeness of movement or object, also furthers the growth of our spirit. Rather than always thinking of the partial, we maintain a focus on the totality of the effort and this promotes the spirit. So often we are engaged in slicing and dicing things into parts. Even as we practice parts of the stroke cycle, we must view this with respect to the whole of the stroke, albeit a shortened whole. We must feel, as well as think. This focus on wholeness brings out inner feelings.

The fortunate man finds a, discipline, that can take one beyond your physical limits, such as sculling, but it could be any activity. The athlete develops from a small self or ego to a more expansive self or spirit. As a coach, you recognize the lessons and education on the water, as the means for expanding this larger self - the larger self-being, the spiritual self.

It is essential that the coach and athlete must be linked in this process. This is why Cerutty ran the sand dunes of Portsea on the Australian Coast with his team, when he was 65 years of age. When the coach trains with his athletes, a bond and a spirit, is developed between coach and athlete.

The Quantum Sculler

  The coach can begin the integral process modestly by engaging a local strength coach, and someone who has expertise in yoga for stretching. A nutritionist can be found and the college strength coach can be enlisted. The major challenge for the coach is laying out this cohesive training program. However, with an integral mindset, laying out this mosaic becomes easier. Then, once initiated, he or she is on a path of learning, implementing and expanding this coaching approach. With this expansion of our knowledge, we are reminded of how much we do not know; we have humility. It becomes clear to coach and athlete that an integral coaching approach takes one into the unknown areas of body, mind and spirit. It is a wonderful odyssey, similar to the early explorers from history, who discovered uncharted waters, we experience immeasurable rewards.

  Sensitive sculling can involve four of our five senses with every stroke. We feel the run of the shell and the invigorating breezes of early spring. We enjoy the various smells emanating from the banks. We see the levelness of our stern and the bubbling effect of the shell's wake. Our subtle touch to the handles eventually becomes masterful including our handling of the sculls with fingers and with flat wrist sculling. However, we must try to stay in touch and connected to nature around us. Recently, I asked a sculler to feel the power of this connection with the earth through the water with a series of strokes.

Through his blades, he was attempting to feel the water as a sphere of energy.

Our sense of touch reaches a deeper level of being because we are seated inches from the water's surface through the flimsy membrane of the shell for long periods of time during our training. We are resurrecting our primordial nature. Where the primates once sat on the earth for extended periods, unfortunately, we now sit on elevated chairs for much of the day. So the rowing seat engages our ancient sensibilities allowing us, as an animal, to operate adeptly, embedded in our earthly cosmology, not on it, but in it. In addition, each time we bury the blades, we are touching the earth. This is eco-sculling. Sitting on the ground, in the shell, or on the floor, returns us briefly to a forgotten state of being. We revive the union between our animate spirit and the earth. The implications of the sculling seat is mainly overlooked because we lack an understanding of the profound importance of sitting in a shell, on the floor, or on the earth's carpet and the benefit to our larger more holistic life.

With good sitting posture and a mindset that thinks upward, we resist the downward pull of gravity, and open ourselves to love of sculling, and indirectly, in a small way, to the love of the Earth. So it is essential for the athletes to have meditative experiences in the fall, late spring, and summer, outdoors on an earthly cushion, and in the winter months on the floor. My crews would follow this practice at the completion of a water

The Quantum Sculler

session in the fall and late spring by retreating to a grassy location next to the boathouse, thoroughly regenerating themselves through this quiet concentration session.

`Sculling provides an excellent opportunity to relate to the Earth through our sitting position in meditation and through relaxed handling of the sculls. We must realize that the water is part of the Earth's outer layer and contains a power to be used. This is a source energy that we can tap into. We embrace all aspects of our immediate environment, our body, the shell, the sculls, the water, and the banks and the environs of the river or lake. We become in the thoughtful words of Thomas Berry, people of the "United Species," as we relate to the local animals that inhabit the shared space, the Beavers, the Deer, the Muskrats, the Otters, the various species of birds, and the peripatetic Canadian Geese. The vision of Ken Wilber mantra progressed from egocentric to ethnocentric and finally to world-centric. Berry is concerned about the state of the Earth, with all of its varied inhabitants, and with the Universe. Berry's view is a large step beyond the world-centric view.

Throughout the year we tap into the power of water, wind, rainfall, snows, numbing cold, unbearable heat of summer, and sleet of late fall and early spring. We learn how to adapt to these conditions. As scullers, we are resilient. We make the necessary adjustments to the weather facing us. The conditions simply become part of us, an easy extension, as amphibians. As such, we embrace the environmental conditions and become part of the natural world. It is an aspect of sculling that has been part of our sport for the past three hundred years, since its early beginning in the 1700s.

This must be part of our spirit training and it begins with our daily Quiet Sitting. We return to a communication with the Earth. We further touch the Earth, the water, through our blades and we recognize that the water is a source of power. This is especially true if we place the blade at blade depth and follow the old adage of "pulling what you can handle." We continue to feel this relationship with the land when we leave the shell. We take a good look around us and view the trees. I see this at the Hobart boathouse that fortunately has a small forest facing it on the far side of the canal. It is alive with birds and animals. We are part of their space and they are part of ours. It only takes a brief moment to glance and feel the awe and wonder of this beautiful green belt. This should be an integral part of our life outside of the shell.

Living in the Finger Lakes Region, this outlook comes easily as the Amish farms are all around us. It is quite apparent that these farmers love the land. It is quite a sight to see a man managing a team of eight large draft horses. We must follow their lead. We must pay close attention to our equipment and how we use this equipment.

The Quantum Sculler

Before the Amish came to this area, there were the Senecas. Similar to all indigenous peoples, they invoked the cosmic forces to sustain their way of living. "The Native American war leader of the Oglala Lakota Sioux, Crazy Horse, invoked cosmic forces to support himself in battle. He knew that those forces resided in the depths of his being and he in them." [61] This is a source of power that we have lost through our lack of daily communication with the natural world.

I always had athletes hug the nearby trees after a long hill run, feeling the girth, the bark and the energy. You had to use your imagination. Two of the larger male athletes went tandem in their tree hugging of one of the bigger trees, and so, added a little mirth to the exercise. Somehow, as athletes, we have to regain this larger consciousness and tap into these cosmic-earth forces that are all around us.

We must also pay close attention to our immediate environment, our bodies. We must feel how the body moves efficiently. This is done specifically with the amount of time we spend on slow motion sculling. You begin to know where you are in this beautiful universe in space and time. You become intimate with the slide bed and relate it to the larger picture of life. You begin to achieve a more cosmological perspective. So, the complete picture of our being includes the whole -- body,

---

[61] Thomas Berry, *The Sacred Universe*, p. 74

equipment and the land. It is an integral picture and the qualitative part of our beautiful sport. It requires deep learning and constant practice. It requires our constant attention to what is around us everyday, both in the shell and out of the shell. We must nourish this attention to the Earth, on a daily basis. We must recognize the cosmic energy that is stored in the Earth. We see that deep spiritual power is as critical to develop in our training as physical power. It comes from relaxation, posture, breathing, our relationship with the natural world, and the full enjoyment of the wholeness process. We must move to a much deeper level beyond the analytical processes of the rational mind. Otherwise, we find ourselves in a world devoid of meaning. This is not the way of the indigenous people throughout the world. Somehow, they have managed to retain their sense of mystery and awe towards the earth and the universe as a whole. In the world of sport, it may be that this is an under-emphasized portion of our planning and programming. We simply overlook the deeper meanings that can be discovered in sport, in rowing and promoted with all ages. We must maintain our ability to dance in and out of the shell.

For the coach and athlete, this mental, physical and spiritual experience has a deeper purpose that optimizes the individual's performance and personal development in the group. We look out for each other. We refrain from judging and simply accept one another as part of a unit. A developed deep empathy produces growth in our consciousness.

Ultimately, training the spirit involves this awareness and deep connection to the natural world. The oarsman is so close to the water, but in some ways so far away. He has to work hard at concentrating to be one with the shell, the oars, and the water. He can't approach the sport as though these are separate units. He must recognize the wholeness of the activity.

Readings from wisdom literature are helpful. The readings can come from a variety of sources including, art, history, biography, literature, poetry, spirituality and ecology. From this, athletes can seek and find the relationships of their reading to their physical activity. This deeper inner transformation of coach and athlete comes from study of Western Transpersonal Psychology, Mind-Science and Eastern Metaphysical literature. Eastern literature benefits from more than 2,500 years of pertinent wisdom addressing the development of self-knowledge. This deeper inner transformation of coach and athlete comes from study of Eastern and Western literature. A good place to begin such study is the writings of Lao Tzu, His Holiness The Dalai Lama, Shunryu Suzuki and a careful reading of Eugen Herrigel's wonderful little book, *Zen in the Art of Archery*. Herrigel's masterpiece is particularly helpful with his detailed exposition of the master's insistence on following the process, rather than focusing on a superficial goal. Herrigel lost sight of the important goal of learning to shoot correctly. By doing so, he also overlooked himself as the real target. The archer gains self-knowledge by focusing on the learning process and not on the target. There are so many lessons to be learned from this little book, including patience, humility, kindness, concentration, and most of all, the importance of the process. All of this can be applied to our learning to scull efficiently with precision.

    Shunryu Suzuki, in his little masterpiece, reminds us to exercise a "Beginner's Mind," a mind that is open and curious. This is wonderful advice for anyone, but especially for the coach and athlete. While the "Expert's Mind" is closed, we must remain young and curious.

    In my sculling coaching, my focus initially is on the whole movement of body and shell. My first lesson from the Old Coach was a masterful presentation of the thirty-two movements of the stroke cycle. It left me with a large headache on my long five-mile bike ride home. Over the years, I have learned from observation of a moving object, that I am looking immediately for the degree of Flow in the Motion, whether it be an athlete, a child, an animal or a performer on stage.

    When I think holistically, I can feel myself marshaling my full inner force from my toes to the crown of my head. To observe the whole tree is an enjoyable and educational visual exercise of unlimited possibilities. The Maple is quite distinct from the Sycamore in terms of leaf shape, trunk configuration, and texture of the bark. But these distinctions come later with study of the individual parts. Our first recognition is that of a tree, or whole object of nature. From this perspective we move to the parts. The trees, lining the street on my route to our downtown, remind me of the unlimited variety in nature and inject a quick boost to my spirit. The world around us is completely integral.

There has to be a grounding and deep embrace of Nature for our spirit to develop and flourish. This involves a lifetime of education for living deeply in nature. Frank Lloyd Wright advised a young architect, "Do not design your house to be built on the top of the hill, but rather just below the top. The house will then be of and in the hill, not merely on it."

George Pocock found religious significance and increased feeling for the nurturing Earth in handling, shaping, and examining wood fragments from the giant cedars in the Northwest. These giants of the forest were something to behold, he wrote, "Some have been growing for a thousand years, and each tree contains its own story of the centuries long struggle for survival." We have to find some aspect of nature that we love, in our education beyond formal academia and relate it to our rowing. For me, it was developing the relaxed relationship between my hands, the wood handles and oars.

The athlete has to be exposed to the outdoors on a regular basis. Consequently, the Hobart and William Smith College students were exposed to the rigors of the Finger Lakes winter on a daily basis. They were encouraged to think they were Vikings. It was the Vikings who crossed the North Atlantic in open boats. The students found that there is nothing more beautiful than experiencing an easy jog in new fallen snow. For a rower to experience the vicissitudes of nature can become a way of life, leading to the expansion of their own spirit. With jogging in the elements, there was always an element of playfulness and healthy banter between running partners. This play easily spilled over to the water workouts through speed play where the stroke length and speed were varied, sometimes with a pre-arranged schedule and sometimes at the whim of the stroke person.

During my college wrestling days, my daily pre-practice warm-up would be a three-mile run around the perimeter of the campus. Since we were situated in the snow belt of Southwestern Ontario, the run was usually accomplished in drifting, biting, snow and the last hill before finishing my run was a slippery, icy climb on all fours - a definite challenge to the spirit. This was my method of touching base with the outside world throughout the long winter. These moments alone are still wonderful memories of the solitude, the cold icy blasts coming from the borders of Manitoba, and the challenge of the drifting snow. It brought out the very best of my inner spirit and resolve.

Percy Cerutty felt immersion in nature was imperative, as his Stotan philosophy was based on communication with nature. He encouraged his athletes not only to train outside on the hills, or on the sands of the nearby beach, but also, to sleep outside under the stars, listen to the birds in the morning, feel the sand between your toes, smell the flowers, and listen to the pounding surf. He felt that he had to get the athletes away from the running track, feel the naturalness of the surrounding environment and operate as free animals. He felt, "that Nature can bring the mind and body into perfect harmony and balance with the universe. This is one of the factors that allows the athlete to reach new levels of excellence." [62]

The athlete's spirit is expressed in the power of his attention or focus and his mindfulness of the immediate environment and the task at hand. Total awareness on the part of the athlete, no matter what he is doing, becomes part of his deeper being and his spirit. To foster and enhance the growth of this spirit, we must have moments of deep reflection.

For a rowing coach, the highly spirited nature of group of athletes in an eight-oared shell, I feel translates into a length improvement over the course of a race. Closer to home, I recall the high spirit of the William Smith women in the 1990's. The athletes' program contained the usual strength, speed, and endurance components combined with quiet sitting, relaxation, visualization, concentration, mindfulness and movement practice. It was a beautiful example of holistic programming. In ten weeks

---

[62] Larry Meyers, *Training with Cerutty*, p.169

Training the Spirit

of winter training, they made great strides with their mental/spiritual training, through their daily quiet sittings and simulation drills without the handle on the ergometer. But it was their high-spirited rowing that was so apparent. Consequently, rival coaches were impressed with their spirit and the consistency of their performance.

The final element in this development of individual and team spirit is respect and freedom in the team. Coach and athlete are co-partners in the overall experience. The athlete is receiving an education from the coach and vice versa. The coach has to listen to this evolved and well-trained athlete. This is where the coach can find information. This type of philosophy allows everyone's individual spirit to grow and share. Under this system of easy exchange of ideas and information, there is no room for the authoritarian coach. The system of training and coaching is completely one of freedom. It goes a long way to moving the athlete beyond the ego, towards a consideration for the World and its people at large.

The mind is viewed as a powerful tool in the development of the athlete. Mental training strategies develop clarity, focus and concentration engaging the mind. Training with empathy and compassion, encompasses the spirit, and provides the groundwork for the whole process. This is the holistic training of the body for smooth, efficient movement.

The Quantum Sculler

Challenges are a wonderful way to release the spirit welling up inside of the athlete. One form of a challenge that was presented to me, as an athlete, was daily high-stroke half-minute pieces. Every stroke had to be monitored for clean and relaxed execution. This was also a mindfulness exercise. As I became more accomplished, my confidence rose, and I became ever more spirited and more eager to improve the performance of the skill and boat speed. For my athletes, I added partial high-stroke pieces and this allowed them to engage in this activity in a playful manner with plenty of water flying.

The exercise that began as a challenge, morphed into a playful, humorous, large splash. People were drenched trying to reach 60 to 70 strokes per minute. The technique was dropped overboard for a few minutes of delight, for a few moments of stretching themselves to reach beyond their limits. An open mind, self-awareness, empathy, letting go, humility, focusing, and mindfulness all play an important part in this growth. These practices go a long way toward developing the complete athlete and the complete coach and their spirit.

Chapter Nine - The Imaginative Mind

Imagination is more important than knowledge. For knowledge is limited to all we now know and understand, while imagination embraces the entire world, and all there ever will be to know and understand.

- Albert Einstein

One of the important qualities of great coaching is having a great imagination. I think George Pocock epitomized this quality. He was not involved with interminable paperwork, and the metrics associated with the modern ergometer. Therefore his imagination was not stifled. His expansive mind concentrated on his boat building, his coaching and his poetry. He valued his command of the English language and his English heritage from the Thames Valley. He was able to see things, because of this vivid imagination, that others failed to see in the athletes' technique and temperament. So, in large part, for the Washington 1936 Olympic Crew, he was the person responsible for placing Joe Rantz in the all-important number seven seat. Pocock, in working with wood, could feel and see the value of the material in his hands. He projected this feel for his materials to life and the athletes themselves.

The Quantum Sculler

The other person, who comes to mind, is the late USA National Team rowing coach, Allen Rosenberg. His imagination surfaced in the vivid metaphors that he employed to describe the stroke cycle. It was his imagination at work, which was influenced by his legal profession and extensive reading. The imagination permits you to see the world differently every day of your life. There are worlds within worlds. On our scale, for coaches there are techniques within techniques for each athlete just waiting to be squeezed out into the open. You only have to see.

"The language of imagination carries humans into a greater understanding of a world of beauty, wonder and intimacy that has a realism far beyond data and measurement." [63] In this respect, there is an impressive array of notables whose footsteps we are following -- Buddha, Taoists, Confucius, Christ, Meister Eckhart, St. Francis of Assisi, Rumi, Crazy Horse, Geronimo, Sitting Bull, Samuel Taylor Coleridge, William Wordsworth, Ralph Waldo Emerson, Rudolph Steiner, John Muir, Rachel Carson, Aldo Leopold, Mahatma Gandhi, Sri Aurobindo, Owen Barfield, Wendell Berry, Pierre Teilhard de Chardin, the incomparable Thomas Berry, George Pocock, and Percy Cerutty. They all relate to the good Earth as a deep source of learning, simplicity, and wisdom. This relationship involves the joining of

---

[63] Carolyn W. Toben, *Recovering a Sense of the Sacred: Conversations with Thomas Berry*, p.99.

The Imaginative Mind

the Earth and their spirit. There is a shift from the linear, analytical and mechanistic to an intuitive, integral and holistic mode of thinking.

This imagination has been a part of me for over 60 years as I try to see the stroke cycle and the run of the shell in my mind, the Mind's Eye. It has been with me since I began to be coached in sculling and wrestling. I had to picture things in my mind. Over time these images became clearer in my mind. I can picture the sculler sliding effortlessly up and down the slide with each stroke using the light trunk swing. We really feel the engagement of the upper trunk at the entry of each stroke and resultant immediate response of the shell under you. This goes a long way to creating Flow. The shell runs under you almost as an independent, intuitive action. It planes level throughout, both of the power and recovery phases and is a fine example of Hanlan's shell "being drawn by a string" when the stroke is executed properly. The level run of the shell is the first quality that I look for in any sculler or crew. Our imagination becomes an important part of who we are and part of our daily living. The Imagination can lead to the ideal athlete, the integrated athlete, where every aspect of training and development is considered- the physiology, the biomechanical, the nutritional, the strength and endurance building, the fine movement training, and the complete mental refinement of the athlete. How do these various sciences interact and integrate to help create a "light," effortless, athletic motion remains the everlasting question? It does require a balanced approach between the rational and the intuitive, and between the conceptual and the experiential.

We, coach and athlete, engage in stretching every aspect of ourselves, including body, mind and spiritual dimensions. We dream; we imagine; we look for the ideal. It is an image that haunts me as it almost seems to be just beyond our perceptual grasp. You can feel and vaguely know it is there and possible, but not quite able to grasp the image and how to achieve it. Such a thinking approach is certainly counter to orthodox coaching.

Michael Wagner, a club coach in Oyster Bay, New York, had these comments: "My experience coaching with Al Borghard, as his assistant, lead me to truly appreciate Al's ability to be very creative each day on how he explained the goals of the workout for the day on land. I virtually never heard Al repeat himself and he always seemed to offer a new way to look at the rowing stroke, a new phrase, a new concept. And he did this every day! I believe this resulted in the athletes being more engaged, whether the athletes realized it or not, because they were being asked each day to look at the rowing stroke in a new and different way, to use their imagination. To be on land listening to Al and trying to picture in their mind's eye how this new idea he is explaining will work out there on the water. Sparking a student's imagination on a daily basis, and this sense of surprise in how the teacher is asking the student to look at the world will lead to a life long appreciation of looking at life through a different lens." [64] This approach reminds me of starting each practice with an ergometer demonstration on some aspect of the stroke. It certainly brought the athletes to a focused and concentrative attention before they went out onto the water.

Imagination and visualization, allow you to see the Sculler's Entry, the glide forward from the hips on the recovery, the smooth five-movement release, and the whole body drive with the salt shaker movement. Visualization is the key to ingraining the movements into your body structure. The coach, also, must engage his imagination in order for the movements to become part of his mind and body. Use of the metaphor becomes extremely important. For example, workers cutting long grass with the two-handed scythe, beside the Canadian National Railway in my youth. This was the perfect analogy for the flow of the movement. Another vivid imaginative image is the slow, steady stream. These illustrative examples give life to the imaginative process. We must revive our youthful ability to project and protect these vivid images. Here reading to children is helpful especially the works of C.S. Lewis and J.R.R. Tolkien. Like experiences surely will surface in our coaching as we set ourselves in a different world. This world does not include the drudgery of paper

---

[64] Correspondence from Michael Wagner

The Quantum Sculler

work, recruiting concerns, adhering to the timelines of the periodization plan, or the overemphasis on the ergometer score. All of these lead to staleness and mundaneness of thought. We are seeking a lively, and imaginative mind for our coaching.

Chapter Ten - Complexity and Consciousness

Complexity is the development of skill. It becomes subtler and subtler. With increased complexity comes increased consciousness. We simply become finer tuned with our skills.

  - Jimmy Joy

Complexity occurs in sculling when you refine the technique. This parallels the stuff and matter of our universe. This is accomplished with specific emphasis on movement training both in and out of the shell. It is viewed as an important training principle that is programmed throughout the training year. This type of training provides the simple objective for all aspects of the training program, achieving smooth, continuous movements. Peter Ralston in his book, *Cheng Hsin: The Principles of Effortless Power*, identifies five factors for achieving this state of effortlessness, "being calm, being relaxed, being centered, being grounded, and being whole and total." [65] This is an excellent guidepost for both training and racing.

This training facilitates all the positive effects of the physiological programing. It opens the awareness of the athlete and

---

[65] Peter Ralston, *Cheng Hsin: The Principles of Effortless Power*

The Quantum Sculler

makes it possible for him to achieve his potential. It is an unusual objective, smooth motions, but it is so critical that this movement training is programed into the daily workouts with specific drills designed to develop the wholeness. It is a reminder that we must go slowly to go fast, and to evolve properly. This specific objective, smooth motion, is often overlooked by contemporary coaches in their quest for higher numbers.

In the fall, concentration is on the integrated drive from the entry to the release (you feel the constant pressure on the blade face) and on the well-timed swing of the trunk from the release to the entry (you feel the movement from the hips throughout the recovery). Refinement is particularly critical for the release and the entry, the transitions. In the winter, movement training continues with detailed work on simulation exercises. Here timing of the various movements can be drilled to be exact. Then in the spring, refinement of the entry and release is repeated. For specific movement of the release, it is the angle of extraction of the blade (45 degrees), the roll or circular movement of the hands and movement of the trunk out of bow following full extension of the arms. For the entry, it is quick and complete coupling of the drop of the blade with the pull. In both cases, the specific movements are part of a whole movement. This drill work on the movements is supported with daily meditation (visualizing the movements) and yoga sessions.

Complexity and Consciousness

This training positively affects the mind, as the consciousness reaches another level of development. Coach and athlete become more attentive, mindful, and concentrated. Of course, these qualities of refined movement spill over into racing, as the stroke cycle reaches an automatic stage of development.

Everything in the cycle is more detailed, precise, refined and because of attention to detail. Thus there is an increase in complexity involved. Consciousness, by athlete and coach, attains a totally new level of performance. A new level of spirit develops in the athlete's commitment to his skill development. This spiritual element pervades his whole approach to the sport and envelops his whole body. At these higher levels of skill and consciousness, it is spiritual. It is an enthusiasm that encompasses his total being. It is an extraordinary feeling of accomplishment. Every coach wants spirited athletes. Roger Bannister proclaimed that the "Human Spirit is indomitable." Out of the shell the athlete's newly developed sense of the spiritual becomes a part of him.

Evolutionary biologists, Lynn Margulis and Elisabet Sahtouris, in their recent research, have discovered example after example of cooperation and sociality in the service of evolution.[66] "There is an increasing trend in evolution of finding that

---

[66] Carter Phipps, *Evolutionaries*, p.83

living organisms increase their capacity to cooperate. To achieve this new level of development, coach and athlete must work together on a cooperative basis. They learn it pays to cooperate. The same principle is involved, whether we are talking about bats, bees, bacteria, or basketball players." [67]

The athlete's physiological body must work on a cooperative basis and not on a competitive model. Within the body, various organs work together as a cooperative unit. Outside the body, muscle and bone structures work in a similar fashion. This is what produces a smooth, continuous flowing action. The athlete operates well within his capabilities for optimal results. He employs a great deal of feel for the proper degree and magnitude in his movements. For the sculler, "he pulls what he can handle." This becomes the beacon of expression for all of his training, on the erg, in the weight room, in his running, and of course, in the shell. He performs with a great deal of muscle cooperation, body and mind control. If he is on a team, it must be cooperation, cooperation, and more cooperation amongst the team members for the best results. This is how any situation evolves optimally, especially the training of a high level athlete. The competitive model that so many athletes and teams use is simply not as effective.

---

[67] Carter Phipps, *Evolutionaries*, p.82

Complexity and Consciousness

The universe is constantly developing towards higher levels of material complexity and subsequently evolves to a higher level of Consciousness. This is a theory of evolution that Teilhard called the Law of Complexity/Consciousness.[68] For Teilhard, this evolution culminated in the Omega Point and he related it to his beliefs. It pointed the way of evolution for him. It became his ideal for the eventual development of the person. For scullers and their coaches, evolution towards a perfected stroke is the ultimate development of the athlete. It includes all aspects of training, especially the evolution of his skilled movements. Everything comes together and achieves David Bohm's "Implicate" physical level, the parts and the whole flow. The athlete unites the various aspects of his training and achieves a level of transcendence as he realizes flow. The feeling of flowing movements pervades the whole body. He unites the rational with the intuitive into a singular action, the being and the becoming.

This coaching approach is totally holistic, cooperative, rational, meditative, and spiritual. It demands attention, deep attention to detail by coach and athletes. It becomes a large part of our being. For the student, it is a second form of education that complements his academic work. It is a culture that goes far beyond the usual coaching and training methods. It requires study and exploration by everyone involved. It is higher level of Con-

---

[68] Teilhard de Chardin, *The Law of Complexity/Consciousness*

sciousness development and it becomes a way of life. As such, it involves evolution of the mind as well as evolution of the body. We are part of the great evolutionary process that sweeps the earth and us with it. He might also, along the way, develop a feel and connection to the Natural World. If so, he can appreciate being a part of a "biocracy." Simply, he becomes an advanced person. He cares about his own nature and the natural world around him. He feels connected and seeks relationships in his sport, his school, and in his workplace. It is a lifelong educational process. He operates with the beginner's mind, as he is constantly curious. We are participating in a new coaching paradigm, as well, in an exciting new state of consciousness. The athlete operates in the *Now* with this union with the cosmos that includes the suspension of time-"present, past, and future are dissolved." [69] With operating in the *Now*, creativity flourishes because we are not dealing with the past. We let go of our old self. In *letting go* of our old selves the athlete can embrace new methods of movement that are more athletic, finer and more complex movements.

Life outside of the shell also witnesses a change in the person. He realizes that he himself is evolving as he keeps pace with the rhythms, natural flow and evolution of the universe. It is something that Taoists, Stoics, and indigenous peoples real-

---

[69] Matthew Fox, *Meister Eckhart*, p.147

ized. This is a totally novel way of looking at sculling. It is more humanistic with the full development of the individual clearly in mind, mental, physical and spiritual. With this approach we are getting into the very marrow of the person.

> Our normal waking consciousness, rational consciousness as we call it, is but one special type of consciousness, whilst all about it, parted from it by the filmiest of screens, there lie potential forms of consciousness entirely different ... No account of the universe in its totality can be final which leaves these other forms of consciousness quite discarded. How to regard them is the question, for they are so discontinuous with ordinary consciousness.
> - William James, *Consciousness Levels*

The movements should be presented in a holistic manner, with the major emphasis being the recovery and the drive. In the latter stages of his development, the sculler focuses on each of the specific movements. He learns to feel the precise pathway of each motion. For the recovery, the focus is the relaxed swing from the hips. The actual details of the release and entry are set-aside, for the time being, for the sake of putting the two wholes together, the recovery and the drive. All of these specific actions relate to whole continuous movement. Total Movement is poetic

The Quantum Sculler

and spiritual, embracing our total being. It is not something that you can quantify. It is quality of movement that you are experiencing and achieving.

We are speaking of an evolution bringing matter and mind together, the without and the within. Consciousness and matter are intrinsically related. As our use of matter becomes more complex, more subtle and refined, our consciousness evolves. For the individual, it is an evolution and a convergence of life and thought, matter and mind; for the sculler, skill and consciousness. We project beyond our set ways. We move beyond, way beyond orthodox teachings. We move well beyond old coaches and writers, Fairbairn and Bourne, but, we touch base with old scullers such as Pearce and Berry. Here is where intrinsic action takes place. After time in the shell, we are able to feel this change occurring in ourselves. We look at the world differently. This is a quantum world of connections and relationships. This is what Joe Rantz had to learn with his 1936 Washington crew. He had to learn to trust the other person. [70]

We begin to be able to see ourselves experiencing a wonderful evolutionary skill. We rapidly project ourselves into the 21st Century. We become the stuff of the universe and the world comes into our consciousness. Evolution allows us to see and feel Matter and Mind coming together.

---

[70] From James Brown's *The Boys in the Boat*

Complexity and Consciousness

With time and practice, these two movements of the Release and Entry become grooved. They begin to take on some semblance of the precision that the sculler will eventually achieve. Relaxation carries over from the Recovery into the Drive phase. All the extra motions are eliminated. The object at this point is to keep hands and fingers relaxed in holding the handles. This relaxation will greatly assist with the progress of improvement for these two movements. By emphasizing the wholeness of these two major movements, the sculler's consciousness rises to another level. There is far less energy expended. The total movement begins to become smoother. The individual actions of the fingers and wrists gradually are more refined. The athlete becomes more confident in his sculling.

Alignment of the body on the seat back-and-front, side-to-side, and up-and-down is also critical. After experimenting with this alignment you relax into the pelvic girdle. A child enjoys his time playing with building blocks and intuitively understands the principles of alignment. The blocks will remain standing if placed directly on top of one another. The human body follows the same principles in sitting; starting with the pelvis, the abdomen and lower back, the chest and upper back, the shoulders and arms, the neck, and finally the head. With these segments stacked directly on top of one another, the body is able to sit in a

The Quantum Sculler

balanced manner. This positioning requires little effort to maintain and permits the major muscles of the body to relax. [71]

When you sit in meditation, breathe in and out with the whole body. Will Johnson, a meditation master from Canada, feels that, "when breath fills the whole body, there is no room for thought to reside." [72] This must be practiced in our sitting, whole body breathing, and inserted into the stroke cycle by inhaling during the drive and breathing out during the recovery. This act of breathing becomes an important part of our individual technique. This specific process of breathing does help to curtail involuntary thoughts. When we incorporate the breathing we are operating at a very different level of Consciousness.

The overall effect on the Consciousness is significant. It simply involves a different way of thinking. You must have an expanded sense of your authentic self. At the same time you feel that your body and movements are completely stripped down to a minimum. You take on an air of sparseness and leanness. You switch your thinking to an integrated and whole mode. You begin to feel that you are melting into the surrounding environment. There is only a sliver of separation between you and the shell and the environment. This "melting into the environment" is easily experienced when you sit in meditation with the eyes

---

[71] Will Johnson, *The Posture of Meditation*, p.20
[72] Will Johnson, *Aligned, relaxed, Resilient: The Physical Foundations of Mindfulness*, p.116

closed. You immediately feel the lack of boundaries between your body and the objects in the room. You experience the absolute rest and joy of your posture. Your spine becomes erect and elongated.

Sensitive sculling can involve four of our five senses with every stroke. We feel the run of the shell and the invigorating breezes of early spring. We see the levelness of our stern and the bubbling effect of the shell's wake. Our subtle touch to the handles eventually becomes masterful, with our handling of the sculls with fingers and flat wrist while sculling. We must try to stay in touch and connected to nature around us. Recently, I asked a sculler to feel the power of this connection with the earth through the water with a series of strokes. The blades are tapping into a sphere of energy.

Our sense of touch reaches a deeper level of being because we are seated inches from the water's surface through the flimsy membrane of the shell for long periods of time in our training. We are resurrecting our primordial nature. Where the primates once sat on the earth for extended periods, unfortunately, we now sit on elevated chairs for much of the day. So the rowing seat engages our ancient sensibilities allowing us, as an animal, to operate adeptly, embedded in our earthly cosmology, not on it, but in it. With good sitting posture, a mindset that thinks upward, we resist the downward pull of gravity, and open ourselves to love of sculling, and indirectly, in a small way, to the love of the earth.

So it is essential for athletes to have meditative experiences in the fall, late spring, and summer, outdoors on an earthly cushion; and in the winter months on the floor. Sitting on the ground, in the shell, or on the floor returns us briefly to a forgotten state of being. We revive the union between our animate spirit and the earth. The implications of the sculling seat is mainly overlooked because we lack an understanding of the profound importance of sitting in a shell, on the floor, or on the earth's carpet and the benefit to our larger more holistic life. For coach and athlete, this mental, physical and spiritual experience has a deeper purpose that optimizes the individual's performance and personal development. The athlete experiences the silence, the solitude, the stillness, and the simplicity of the mind and body in a full state of deep concentration.

It is this sense of touch experienced through our connection to seat, oar handles and our feet on the foot stretchers, not only the balls of the feet, but also, the inner and outer edges of the feet and the heels. Lately, I had the college lads rowing without their sneakers to experience feeling more with the feet.

A negative ego inhibits us from communicating with our shell in the present. This is the ego that is self-serving and concerned about matters that only pertain to me. In seeking to change, we must strive to empty our mind of all this harmful thinking so that we can start to become one with our boat and the water surrounding us. We are in the process of *'letting go"* when we do this practice. When we do speak of ego, we refer to the fact that it is not self-centered or measuring. Rather, it is expansive, positive, and humble. When we elevate our being, we elevate our consciousness, and consequently, our performance improves.

Ego recognizes that things and people are connected. The world that we live in is whole. It is a world-centric quality that the individual embraces. Thus tolerance, justice, and empathy are key ingredients to the athlete's personality. Once the concentration on self leaves our minds, we can replace it with a deep focus on the present. Now we are just doing and moving in the world that surrounds us.

Higher consciousness and awareness are achieved by feeling your body through the movements with a deep concentrated awareness for their intricacies. This is achieved by slow motion sculling. Your consciousness is connected with the various movements. By using slow motion, gradually more of the pathways are moving towards Bohm's implicate level of operating. It is subtlety of movement that is developing.

It is imperative that we touch base with our deeper nature through our daily meditation sessions. This should be a habitual practice of touching base with our inward self, something that is part of our nature that we look forward to experiencing. In doing this practice, we become more attentive, more aware. Sri Aurobindo, a thinker, political activist and mystic, whom Indians revered with Ghandi, had tremendous powers of concentration and could sit and study in the same position all night long. He felt that through meditation you learned to become "an explorer of the planes of consciousness." One of the most serious obstacles he had to conquer was to learn to silence the endless chatter of thoughts that flow through the normal mind. You had to discover in his words, "the new country within in us and to do this we had to learn how to leave the old country behind." [73]

    The practice of sitting can be performed before a piece. Fifty years ago, Old Coach Fitzpatrick had me pause before a work piece on the water and sit quietly for a couple of minutes. He also had me do it after a practice session. This past spring, I gave the same advice to the Hobart varsity coxswain to use with his crew at the 2015 Intercollegiate Rowing Association Championships. They could do this sitting before the start of the race. The development of our consciousness has specific practices and modes of thinking as outlined below: The sculler has to leave "the old country" of fragmentation behind, and embrace integration and wholeness.

---

[73] Michael Talbot, *The Holographic Universe*, p. 263

Complexity and Consciousness

Sri Aurobindo also had this to say about wholeness: "that in the great and luminous kingdoms of the Spirit, is that all separateness is an illusion, and all things are interconnected and whole. It is as one descends from the higher vibrational levels of reality to the lower that a progressive law of fragmentation takes over. We fragment things because we exist at a lower level of vibration of consciousness and reality." [74] These comments by Aurobindo are indistinguishable from the thoughts of David Bohm. It was the spiritual universe within, that Bohm was concerned with reaching. For Bohm, the implicate level "could equally be called Idealism, Spirit, Consciousness." [75] Our approach to sculling should begin to reflect this world, as we experience more refinement of the Movements. We are reaching a much higher vibrational plane. Our consciousness is definitely influenced by skill development.

From the chapter on Meister Eckhart in *The Transformation of Nature in Art*, Ananda Coomaraswamy writes: "There was a time when Europe and Asia could and did actually understand each other very well. Asia has remained herself; but subsequent to the extroversion of the European consciousness and its preoccupation with surfaces, it has become more and more difficult for European mindset think in terms of unity, and therefore

---

[74] Michael Talbot, *The Holographic Universe*, p.262.
[75] Michael Talbot, *The Holographic Universe*, p.273.

more difficult understand the Asiatic point of view ... Eckhart presents astonishing close parallel to Indian modes of thought, some whole passages and many single sentences read like a direct translation from Sanskrit."

We can easily insert American for European. So this is our current problem with the movement training that we are trying to instill on a much smaller scale of importance. We are trying to think and teach wholeness to students who think and are educated in parts. Can it become a way of life? Can we have that much influence in our coaching? It certainly was for Meister Eckhart and his contemporary brother in philosophy, Ananda Coomaraswamy. It is an ambitious undertaking for the crew coach but the nature of this sport has in the past lent itself to this approach as evidenced by the Thames Watermen.

Every aspect of sculling takes on a quality of lightness, and wholeness, and it becomes pure joy to scull. This beautiful endeavor involves both the mind and the body. Movements become effortless. There is no struggle in the sculler's mind as he perfects his timing and his subtle execution of the release and the entry. The blade slides into and out of the water at each end of the slide. At this stage, the sculler approaches becoming an artist. His sculling is an art form.

With higher levels of consciousness and attention to detail, the sculler should be aware of the controlled swing from the hips, the quick hold of the entry by the shoulders, the even-

Complexity and Consciousness

power application on the blades during the Drive; and the easy flow of the Release and follow-through. Attention is total awareness. It is not the same as concentration, which is exclusive. Attention is inclusive and we become aware of both the outward things and the inward things. Krishnamurti refers to this way of looking as "choice less awareness". With this method, you are never judging yourself. It "means watching without choice." [76]

This all-encompassing awareness should also include seeing the firm quality of movement of the shell's stern. Attentive awareness takes in everything, both in and out of the shell. Consciousness emphasizes thinking whole. We have to live our life in and out of the shell as an exercise in Wholeness. It becomes part of our greater spirit. Wholeness in sculling begins with our relationship with the equipment - sculls and shell. We should treat the equipment with care and respect. Too often, I see equipment thrown down on the dock, rather than being carefully placed. Next comes our approach to entering and disembarking from the shell. We place one foot onto the track, holding onto the handles with one hand. Then with one foot on the edge of the dock we push off and move that foot from the dock directly into the foot stretcher and, at the same time, sit down on the seat. Then we place the second foot into the stretcher. All of this is completed in one athletic movement. These movements have to

---

[76] Krishnamurti, *Freedom from the Known*, p.33.

The Quantum Sculler

be performed every time we enter the shell and done with the very best of our athleticism. We must be completely aware of the exactness of these movements.

In Jean Gebser's structure of Consciousness, our history has moved from the Archaic Period to the Magical, to the Mythical and Mental Periods. Now, after thousands of years of transitional progression, we finally are becoming more Integral (arational, aperspectival, integral), and more whole. It is a positive demonstration of the evolution of our consciousness. Gebser [77] actually experienced a little known instance of "Satori", while he was visiting Sarnath in 1961, where Guatama the Buddha had preached his inaugural sermon. Gebser writes about this experience, "It was a sober, on the one hand, happening with crystal clarity in everyday life, which I perceived and to which I reacted 'normally'. On the other hand, and simultaneously being a transfiguration and irradiation of the indescribable, unearthly, transparent 'Light' -- no ecstasy, no emotion, but a spiritual clarity, a quiet jubilation, a knowledge of invulnerability, a primal trust. Since Sarnath, I am as if recast, inwardly, since then everything

---

[77] The story of consciousness pandit, Jean Gebser, is worth taking a moment to consider, recalling that Gebser had to move in the 1930s and early 1940s from his native Germany to Spain, to France, and then to Switzerland. He was assisted in avoiding execution and leaving Spain, by poet Federico García Lorca. Gebser then escaped from France a bare two hours before the closing of the borders. His philosophy (Consciousness Development) and views on history would not have been well-received by the Nazi occupiers.

is in its proper place and it continues to take effect and is in a way an irradiation that is always present and at hand." This represented the culmination of his long struggle and labor, until his death in 1973, to achieve an arational, aperspectival and integral consciousness. In his arational integral consciousness, the fixed position of ego is transcended and goes beyond the dualistic thinking of the world and thus beyond mere reason and its linear perceptivity. We become ego-free and hence aperspectival. That is to say, not transfixed in partial viewpoints. [78]

Eventually the consciousness level of the sculler should be one of feeling immanent and transcendent. Both qualities are present in the Flow involved with specific movements of the entry. Immanence is the more superficial aspect, the feeling of the various movements. Transcendence represents the deeper aspect, the whole continuity of this easy movement. The latter is where movement becomes intuitive. This is the flow of the movement. Eventually, flow transitions to a deep state of awareness. It almost becomes spiritual in nature. The sculler achieves a relationship to the immensity of the universe and its qualities of continuous change. He begins to recognize the changes in his own being and relates those changes to the world around him. He realizes that the line is thin between the leaf, the tree and the surrounding atmosphere. Where is the demarcation

---

[78] Georg Feuerstein, *Structures of Consciousness*, p.212

point? He feels that his body is experiencing the same relationship with the thin line between himself the shell and the water. This is a progressive upward spiraling process of development for athlete and coach.

1. Developing comfortability with the sitting position including good posture and breathing techniques. This leads to improved levels of listening. There is a strong correlation between the ears, posture, and the overall muscle tone of the body.
2. Recognizing the immediate benefits of developing patience, control of body and mind, and stillness in oneself.
3. Recognizing how these qualities benefit one's life and sculling.
4. Beginning to recognize the power developed inside oneself that parallels the power developed externally by physical training.
5. Recognizing, through Consciousness Training, how we are all connected and rely on one another. We cannot achieve this alone. Wives, loved ones, family, other athletes, our teachers and mentors, and our coaches, all contribute to our success.
6. We develop the ability to remain in the present moment. Time becomes cyclical rather than linear.

7. We begin to develop a quiet, humble, and egoless strength. It is one of understanding, caring, and empathy. Quite a contrast to the usual aggressive approach.
8. We become accustomed and conditioned to sitting for longer periods with a focus on developing attention.
9. We embrace our surroundings and the natural world. We are deeply ecological in our outlook on life.
10. The mind becomes steady, calm and non-attached and non -judgmental.
11. We maintain balance and harmony between thinking, breathing and sensing. This is *Sattva*, from the ancient Vedic tradition of wisdom. It relates to creativity.
12. The union between stillness of the body and stillness of mind becomes a deeply felt experience. This has profound carry-over value for aspects of life - education and occupational.
13. We use the whole body breathing to eliminate the involuntary thoughts.

Each of these of these items above can serve as a Mantram or focus for your daily sitting practice. You simply concentrate on one of these items.

As our consciousness evolves, we become more open and reach higher levels of absolute freedom. Our minds, in doing so, become less cluttered and simpler, patient, and fair. We have then attained much higher levels of existence and operation.

This is truly a state of freedom. We are no longer embroiled in whatever situation that confronts us on a daily basis. We are quite capable of stepping back to observe situations and evaluate our position on items confronting us. It provides our minds some space to evaluate, to contemplate; time to move more slowly. We are more patient, more peaceful, and more simplistic in our living habits. We are more generous; and embrace all ethnic, religious, and national groups of people. There exists a facility and plasticity of mind, body, and spirit. It is a peaceful power of being. In our sculling, this state is displayed through subtle, light, relaxed, and smooth movements. There is no straining to what we are doing in or out of the shell. There is no violence to the stroke cycle. However, the cycle is naturally aggressive in its continuous fluid motion. This spills over to a higher rate of striking over the racing course from start to finish. It is Ghandian Principles applied to sporting activity. Obviously, daily meditation greatly facilitates this mode of operating.

We begin to assume the ancient role of the Warrior, which simply means that, as a sculler, we are brave. The process is not about winning. It is all about the personal development of the athlete when he is attempting to become a Warrior.

Chapter Eleven - Conservation

Our normal waking consciousness, rational consciousness as we call it, is but one special type of consciousness, whilst all about it, parted from it by the filmiest of screens, there lie potential forms of consciousness entirely different ... No account of the universe in its totality can be final which leaves these other forms of consciousness quite discarded. How to regard them is the question, for they are so discontinuous with ordinary consciousness."
- William James

Jean Giono opens his beautiful little book, *The Man Who Planted Trees*, with this remarkable paragraph, addressing the human potential, "For human character to reveal truly exceptional qualities, one must have the good fortune to be able to observe its performance over many years. If this performance is devoid of all egoism, if its guiding motive is unparalleled generosity, if it is absolutely certain that there is no thought of recompense and that in addition, it has left its visible mark upon the earth, then there can be no mistake."[79] The protagonist, a veteran of World War I, decides after the war to plant trees. By doing

---

[79] Jean Giono, *The Man who Planted Trees*, p.7

so, he restores a complete region of war torn France.

Giono's book is a study in conservation and simplicity in a number of ways, including the value of tree planting as a solitary pursuit, the resultant effect on the environment and the towns, and most importantly, how the old man conducts his simple life. This is the other message from Giono, the importance of simplicity in developing economy in Movement and in our lives that parallels our movements in the shell. We are then a complete person. Our deepest example of this nature in rowing was the life of the late Harry Parker. Harry was the complete and devoted coach. He had been well schooled by Joe Burk at the University of Pennsylvania and followed this model throughout his life in coaching.

Simplicity is a first principle. In this case, it is our deep bond with our environment. Our immediate landscape is our body. The athlete has to feel conservation going on within his movements. This is a deeper sense of being; there is no wasted effort. It provides a host of feelings such as awareness, patience, control and confidence. In observing the skilled athlete, these qualities are very apparent. This is not something that you can stage on the moment. It is either a part of your being or not.

Simplicity is achieved by slowing down. By doing slow motion every day, we carve out the unnecessary movements. The whole stroke cycle becomes a picture of absolute slow motion sculling. Through this slow motion, we come to know the cycle more intimately. We experience more of the feel of the Movements. Using and thinking the whole of Movement involves simplicity and conservation in motions. The Movements become easier and you use less energy to do more, "*Multum in Parvo' - Much in Little."* [80]

The coach pours his heart and soul into teaching sculling. He insists upon mastery of each movement with the purpose of achieving Flow and economy of Movement. His single dedication to the art of sculling never fails to impress anyone who was fortunate to spend a few hours with such a coach and person. The parallels between the sculling coach and Giono's protagonist resonate with me. One heals the external environment and the other restores and heals the immediate environment of the body. The fictional person heals and restores the extended environment of rivers, streams, desolate villages and their inhabitants. Both work with their hands, the sculling coach to effectively describe the rowing stroke, and the old man to plant trees. Both men experience similar lives as planters of seeds.

---

[80] Wendell Berry, *Harlan Hubbard*, p.29

The Quantum Sculler

The beloved 18th century Japanese poet, Ryokan, pinpoints probably the major source of our problems – our lack of simplicity in living and our pre-occupation with doing:

> My hut lies in the middle of a dense forest;
> Every year the green ivy grows longer.
> No news of the affairs of men,
> Only the occasional song of a woodcutter.
> The sun shines and I mend my robe:
> When the moon comes out, I read Buddhist poems.
> I have nothing to report, my friends.
> If you want to find the meaning, stop chasing after so many things [81]

When I speak of conservation and simplicity, I am reminded of the words of the American writer Wendell Berry in describing his good friend Harlan Hubbard of Payne Hollow, Kentucky. "The definition of the truly simple man does not precisely fit Harlan Hubbard, whose struggle against the modern world is evidence enough that he was not free of its complications, but it certainly does describe the idea that governed his

---

[81] John Stevens, translator, *One Robe, One Bowl: The Zen Poetry of Ryokan*, p.42

struggle. His effort was to move backward along a line of technological development toward a complex practical orientation to the landscape, an effort that necessarily shaped his economic life, but also profoundly influenced his thought and his art. Harlan unified and simplified his life and character principally by reuniting in his own life many of the modern divisions of labor. The list of disciplines, in which he acquired at least competence and sometimes mastery, is remarkable not only for its length, but for its integrity. He knew and practiced the arts of carpentry, masonry, gardening, goat husbandry, beekeeping, woodcutting, fishing, river navigation (He lived on the banks of the Ohio River), drawing, painting, printmaking, music-making and writing. [82]

This is an ambitious model to follow, but it is important to be aware of what Harlan achieved in his lifetime. He lived the life that Henry David Thoreau wrote about. What Wendell Berry forgot about Harlan Hubbard, was his skill with two oars in a rowboat on the tricky Ohio River or near his Payne Hollow homestead. He had to be skillful to manage the crossing that he had to make on numerous occasions. It became a source of pride to Harlan as he adeptly handled the boat.

For me, simplicity and conservation all begins with slowing down and getting the timing of life's events sequenced

---

[82] Wendell Berry, *Harlan Hubbard*, p.28.

properly. So for sculling, it is slow motion exercise that becomes so critical for our minds and bodies. It ensures that the body is unified and the Quantum Level is touched ever so briefly.

The British Scholar, Martin Lings said, "The truly simple man is an intense unity. He is complete and whole hearted, not divided against himself." [83] This is a wonderful quotation and has been a beacon and source of inspiration for me over the years. Simplicity and unity are the values that we strive for in life and with our sculling. These are important touchstones for the coach, the athletes, and the common man.

We must learn to concentrate on a few things in our lives. With this concentration the dedicated coach will have the proper approach to his coaching and to his life. It will be a life of simplicity and conservation.

It is critical that we look at the whole man while observing our lives both in and out of the shell, to evaluate the degree of simplicity in how we conduct ourselves. Should we not consider doing one thing well in our lives? Should this one thing be something that betters the welfare of others? Buddhists refer to such a pursuit as Right Livelihood. Sculling and rowing coaches can choose to live simply, to focus their energies and to devote a major portion of their lives to assist young scullers in becoming proficient in the skills and art of sculling.

---

[83] Martin Lings, *Ancient Beliefs and Modern Superstitions*, pp.12-13.

In modern society, we pride ourselves in being busy. In addition, the modern advertising industry has bombarded our minds with supposed needs. Our lack of simplicity in living, along with our preoccupation with doing, prevents us from being. This type of lifestyle, with its high consumption levels, remains a challenge in the West for those who want to live simply. It requires that we stay vigilant. Possibly, to counteract this cultural trend, in our lives, we should strive to focus on doing one singular thing well. Moreover, ideally, this one thing should be something that improves the welfare of others.

There is little in the literature of sport scientists that address this phenomenon of energy conservation. Certainly, as the physiologists indicate, improvement in skill leads to internal efficiency. This is where exterior movements have a pronounced bearing on inner functioning. However, in addition, I believe an integrated program that includes both science and emphasizes the art of coaching, leads to training that is more effective. Such programming incorporates both inner and outer dimensions of athletic training. It includes an external component, the rational, as well as the inner mystical.

From the outset, such qualities as patience, slowing down, observation, attention, listening, feeling and controlled movement, when inserted into training, spark the development of the internal athlete.

The Quantum Sculler

These important inner qualities in the athlete are immeasurable, and have a significant effect on their performance. The ancient Chinese Taoists understood the importance of our inner dimension. "Thirty spokes converge upon a single hub. It is on the hole in the center that the use of the cart hinges. We make a vessel from a lump of clay. The empty space within the vessel makes it useful. We make the doors and windows for a room; but the empty spaces make the room livable. Thus while the tangible has advantages, it is the intangible that makes it useful." [84]

It stands to reason that this intangible quality is found only in skilled athletes. In the modern era, we are obsessed with winning, measurement, definition, analysis, and the external. This comes at the expense of the internal and the quality of the experience. Our inner selves become neglected. The intangibles include the quality of the movement, especially economy, and our personal development of- courage, integrity, and persistence.

Many times, the athlete is striving with too much direct effort toward a goal that is usually winning. "All of our discipline, sheer grit and the lust to win may yet get in our way." [85] The indirect approach of concentrating on intangibles falls into

---

[84] Lao Tzu, *Tao Te Ching*, XI, p.27
[85] Sophy Burnham, *For Writers Only*, p.31

neglect. A former Yale athlete, Art Wilmarth, expresses similar concerns as he sees the disastrous effect on our deeper being, "I strongly endorse your emphasis of the qualitative over the quantitative. In our increasingly noisy, hyperactive, greedy world, there is a mania for quantitative 'bottom-line' results based on 'objective' measures of 'productivity.' Of course, every system based on quantitative results can be gamed and subverted (e.g., Enron). Due to the current focus on the 'bottom line', the qualitative aspects of creativity, insight, character, and honest effort are largely ignored. I am always amazed to see everyone walking around with cell phones plastered to their ears. Few people want to engage in reflective thought on the meaning of their lives, the ethical implications of their actions, and other broader issues that should engage their attention." [86]

The practice of sport entails many elements of conservation in all various movements of the body. It is definitely possible to be more efficient in the mind, in the physical body and in our spirit. Movement encompasses both the production and saving of energy. For rowing, as with other sports, movement means emphasizing both qualities, producing and conserving throughout the stroke cycle. The production of energy requires the sophisticated feel for the correct amount of energy to be expended. Conservation encompasses simplicity, smooth muscle

---

[86] From personal correspondence with Art Wilmarth, March 2005

action, slower motions, and the level running of the shell. These ingredients are all interrelated. In the world of nature, wolves, coyotes, and foxes conserve energy with their basic locomotion, loping along in a beautiful relaxed manner -- harmonically rhythmic. [87] This is similar to George Pocock advocating harmony, balance, and rhythm in our movements. It is more natural.

In a like fashion, to conserve physical energy, the athlete develops simple, fluid movements. To conserve the mind, the athlete improves his concentrative ability. To conserve the spirit, the athlete becomes more patient, and controlled. In addition, he is not as goal oriented, which benefits his spirit.

There must be a mental intensity of effort, mindfulness, or staying in the present, in all three of these major areas of our being – the mind, the body, and the Spirit. This quality of mindfulness is a major objective for all practice sessions. It requires concentrated preparation for practice in order to reset the athlete's organism, to have the body in a state of readiness. This may mean having the athletes take a few minutes to do some quiet sitting before they begin the practice.

This single-minded effort establishes the mindset of staying in the present. This quality of mindfulness emerges as the major objective for all practice sessions. A helpful step for developing this heightened attention requires slowing the pace of our

---

[87] Jon Young, *What the Robin Knows*, p.12

life. This goes back to selecting a simpler lifestyle - walk more, read more, take time for quiet reflection. Both quiet sitting and slow motion rowing foster these qualities. Quiet sitting originated from both Eastern and Western sources. Parmenides, the Phoenician philosopher, employed this practice as an effective healing process over 2,500 years ago. For the athlete, quiet sitting is an excellent method for stress reduction and focusing. Too often, we reject or dismiss the Eastern practices because of our lack of exposure to this ancient knowledge. Further, because of our cultural imperialism, supposedly, our education contains all the answers.

We simply have to ingrain the quality of slowness in our lives. The simple man is an accurate description of the famous Canadian Ned Hanlan, regarding his approach to sculling. Hanlan demonstrated this simplicity with a quality of effort and efficiency in his approach to sculling. His lifestyle on Toronto Island reflected his personal qualities and nature as one of the first great spirits and masters of Flow in sculling. He lived, played and rowed on the Island. The island location, a quiet place, was an ideal site for him to perfect his sculling skills, as well as to enjoy a slower-paced life, away from the bustle of the city. This successful athlete possessed an oneness of body, spirit and mind, not only in the shell, but also in life. This non-dual approach completed the athlete, becoming more efficient in his movements, because the distinctions disappeared between sport and life.

To conserve physical energy, the athlete develops simple and fluid movements. You discover simplicity in the total movement and in movement of the parts. For example, by using the fingers in holding the oars, by keeping the wrists flat, with the shoulders remaining level and with little movement of the head, the stroke resembles a simple cyclical pattern. The work of the trunk and legs also follow an efficient design. At the entry, when the body was at full extension, the production of an effective entry is emphasized with the blade positioned at blade depth in the water. You can observe movements of hands and wrists. Hands rise slightly, then you start the pull and wrists rise. This action requires quick sequencing and imparts a definite rhythm to this subtle action of hands and wrists.

In the stroke cycle, obvious ways for conserving energy emerges, especially during the recovery phase. The trunk moves easily from the hips, from extension of the body to extension of the trunk at full reach. The trunk moves constantly changing the angle as the seat moves forward.

Additionally, economic movement surfaces during the drive or power phase as well. During the drive, the extension of the arms move fluidly to flexion, the legs push fluidly from flexion to extension, and the trunk describes a subtle arc over the full length of the slide, while keeping the shoulders level. The three movements are performed with a high degree of relaxation and no straining. The flow of these three prominent movements produces efficient and economical power. The shell runs more effectively and the athlete feels the exhilaration of the shell run. Arm action is the most difficult of the three movements to get correctly without "yanking" the oar handle as you complete the drive. The movement has to be a fluid transition from extension to flexion. Moreover, these are not two separate operations. The production and conservation of energy, when integrated into one fluid action, produces efficient movement. The saving of energy complements production. It is important to recognize, "as you become more skillful at performing an exercise, the energy demands for the exercise are reduced. You become more efficient." [88] Too often, only the former, energy production, merits consideration in sport training.

A former William Smith varsity oarswoman, Collegiate, US and Canadian Champion, Amy Wettergreen Smack has witnessed the negative aspects of too much emphasis on effort, "The concept of conserving energy in rowing and other sports is not reinforced anywhere in our athletic culture! There is so much wasted effort. You see it everywhere, straining, pushing, tensing, and tightening. The 'no pain, no gain' attitude is pervasive. Athletes think it has to hurt (in the sense of the tight, tense muscles working against each other) in order to validate their

---

[88] Martin Lings, *Ancient Beliefs and Modern Superstitions*, pp.12-13.

effort."[89]

Amy was a very efficient athlete with a tremendous sense of purpose, determination, persistence and courage. Consequently, she was able to extract the most out of her smaller body, her mind, and her indomitable spirit.

Another excellent example of mastery training was my experience with wrestling. It became very important to master a few skills well. The wrestler must be sensitive to both his own body and that of his opponent. Consequently, he is very aware of this conserving his power. He knows how to make his opponent work and expend energy. At the same time, he conserves himself.

In a related situation from the workplace, a Canadian friend Mel Ruller, a former project manager for a large construction firm, was confronted with a worker, who his colleagues thought to be unproductive. After a day of careful scrutiny, Mel concluded that the worker was highly efficient and made his various tasks look easy. He was more productive than other workers. His approach to completing his work was based on simplicity of movement. Through Mel's thoroughness and appreciation for energy efficiency on the job, he saved the person's position. The coach must also possess this same deep attention to the details in his athletes' movements as he observes and

---

[89] Correspondence from Amy Wettergreen Smack, July 2005

helps the athlete modify his physical actions in the direction of a more economical pattern.

It is important to acknowledge the web of life, that many things are connected and integrated. We can learn from the simplest experience and apply it to something more serious and elevated. This is such an important part of a coach's responsibility, his ability to place the sport into an educational context. Broadening our horizons beyond sport, helps with our understanding of the impact that the sculling experience can have on the athlete's life. This broader perspective on life by the athlete, also assists the coach with his own personal development and skill acquisition. This type of integrated education leads to a greater plasticity in the brain.

The golf swing, with its inherent rhythm, pace and effortlessness, is the one movement that encapsulates this quality of energy conservation and efficient power. We can also find this attention to detail, accuracy and rhythm in the baseball swing of Joe DiMaggio or Ted Williams. They considered themselves artisans as they worked to perfect their batting skills. Williams would apply this diligence and concentration to perfecting his skills in fly-fishing and he was a dedicated skilled artist throughout his whole life. He studied, applied and taught the effective swing in baseball. You can find the same dedication in all artists, musicians, dancers, the sculptors, writers, potters as well as athletes. So for the artist, there is always an overall concern about conservation of energy or the right power, perfection and mastery. Conservation becomes an important training principle, as "the conservative is someone who seeks to conserve," [90] This is achieved largely through simplifying movements.

The fundamental meaning of Conservation applies effectively to the practice of sport. This principle triggered strong memories from my own sculling and my involvement in other sports. In the embryonic stages of sculling, I recall how the Old Coach stressed simplicity, smoothness, and economy. The sculler had to learn the various movements of the stroke cycle achieving body, blade and boat efficiency through mastery training. A significant part of his method was the practice of conserving energy through a simple and rational stroke cycle. Every body part was exactly positioned and moved efficiently. Every movement had a logical and economic foundation. From the very beginning, the subtlety of action was stressed as you attempted to master each of the movements. Smoothness, simplicity, and economy were drilled into your mind.

. Promoting conservation as a training principle highlights its importance for the athlete. Whole practices can be devoted each week for the development of this quality in the individual stroke cycle. It entails being one with the shell, not straining or

---

[90] Titus Burkhardt, *The Essential Titus Burkhardt*, p.180

pushing, but achieving an easy movement forward and back on the slide. Meanwhile, the seat, riggers, and the whole shell become a unified part with you. This is your immediate environment. You blend with nature. You embrace natural elements of shifting wind and water.

Turns at each end of the slide become more efficient and subtle. Wrist action is minimized and there is more flow to the movement of hands. The body swing is intimately connected to the run of the shell with the decks at each end of the shell remain level. The key for swing is timing of body and seat on the recovery. It is perfection with the slide action being an economic, well-timed, and light movement. You sit lightly and erect on the seat. Achieving this subtle action on the recovery becomes a major focus of the training. We must shift from our analytical mind to an intuitive, feeling mind, sensing seat movement relative to trunk swing.

Conservation is extremely difficult to quantify, as it is governed by intangibles of feeling, sensing, patience, slowing down and overall development of spirit in order to achieve it. You have to engage the spirit of the learning process. In modern sport practice, we are so intent on the mastery and development of the physical, that we overlook the subtlety of executing movements for efficiency and flow. Your thinking must encompass the whole body and mind, much like the animals. Mind and body are not split, but are one. There are no separate parts, no preparation for a movement. The movements are reflexive. Foremost in your mind is the Whole. We learn to observe closely, contemplate, and study our environment. The athlete and coach are groomed to be more like an animal and more in touch with nature, a return to a primordial state of being.

The development of fluid motion requires excellent posture, stressed both in and out of the shell. I encouraged the athletes to be aware of their standing, sitting, walking and running positions. Bill Bowerman, the legendary track coach at the University of Oregon felt, "that good posture was essential for good body mechanics." In addition, high degrees of relaxation and flexibility, exquisite timing and rhythm, are all important factors for refining the various movements. All of this involves hours of practice, openness, and a deep awareness of both the exterior and interior qualities of our athletic being. When we speak of practice, we refer to yoga, rowing at slow motion, good technique in weight training and body weight exercises, core-training, rope jumping for rhythm, careful attention to our running form, and finally good posture for our meditative practices. I recall watching the British four in 1998 doing their jog down to the start of Henley and back to the Leander club. They were four very large, relaxed and thoroughly coordinated athletes doing their pre-practice stretch of four kilometers of easy jogging.

With good technique in lifting, the athlete reinforces his coordination, flow and accuracy. Diversity and variety in the practice format is critical for learning the sensitivity required to be a highly skilled athlete. This is also a balanced and integral approach to training and coaching. This is exceptional quality training and practice at work.

For years I have "toyed" with the goals of mental training or at best, the methodology. After reading Marcus Aurelius' *Meditations*, I agree with Percy Cerutty that Stoicism has a lot to offer in providing direction with one's athletic life. The ancient Stoics gave some extensive guidance for living the simple natural life and the role of perseverance in obtaining such a life. The Spartans led the way with this philosophical way of living and the study of Marcus Aurelius' *Meditations* is an extremely helpful guide. The role of developing our individual perseverance is critical for our inner mental development. Perseverance and mindfulness are keys for developing our mental training. This philosophy is really a "way of Life". You live in the Now, and see the Whole of things. You have to know yourself and realize the critical importance of persevering in the face of obstacles and impediments. Spartan youth were subjected to a very austere lifestyle early in their lives. They learned to persevere in the face of extreme conditions. Percy Cerutty was well aware of this Spartan lifestyle, when training his athletes. Thus he labeled his training method, "Stotan". It is the combination of Stoicism and Spartanism. I designate training as "Spirintel", the marriage between the spirit and intelligence. The spirit embraces the now and the whole. Intelligence selects simplicity of life's choices and perseverance to follow these choices.

Simplicity of Movements, training and simple style of living are important ingredients for an effective culture to be established. It is a culture that is lasting and enjoyable. We have to carefully monitor our simplicity in everything that we do. We must be vigilant as we attempt to ensure that our life simply flows from moment to moment.

Chapter Twelve - Simplicity

Simplicity is a first principle and in this case, it is our deep bond with our environment. Our immediate landscape is our body. The athlete has to feel conservation going on within his movements. This is a deeper sense of being, and it provides a host of feelings, such as awareness, patience, control and confidence. In watching the skilled athlete, these qualities are very apparent. This is not something that you can stage on the moment. It is either a part of your being or not.

- Jimmy Joy

"Western man is rational and Eastern man irrational. The scientific thinking of Europe is founded in rational thought. In the East, the foundation is in the heart and its inspiration, which to the Western mind, with its emphasis upon the intellect, must appear very strange. Eastern man jumps to his conclusion on the wings of intuition, whereas Occidental man arrives at his by a steady progression of intellectual steps. From this causation, man of the West brought the age of the machine, while the man of the East is still largely dependent on the hand."[91]

There is little doubt that for the athlete and especially for rowers, skillful hand actions are of critical importance. To conserve energy, these intangible qualities, are the starting point for the development of effective movements.

I have never forgotten lessons derived from my mentor at Wesleyan University, the late Dr. Eugene Golub. He said that when your mind gets dense with thought, go down into the basement and work with your hand tools. For that interval, you set rationality to one side to provide a moment of rest for your mind.

The practice of sport entails many elements of conservation in all various movements of the body. It is definitely possible to be more efficient in the mind, in the physical body and in our spirit. Movement encompasses both the production and saving of energy. For rowing, as with other sports, movement means emphasizing both qualities, producing and conserving throughout the stroke cycle. The production of energy requires the sophisticated feel for the correct amount of energy to be expended. Conservation encompasses simplicity, smooth muscle action, slower motions, and the level running of the shell. These ingredients are all interrelated.

---

[91] Yanagi, Soetsu, *The Unknown Craftsman*, p.124

Chapter Thirteen - Slow Motion Movement

"At the Battle of Trafalgar, a British naval ship engages a French vessel at close quarters. A French sniper, hidden in the rigging, eventually pins down the British crew. John Franklin, the Arctic explorer, watches his shipmates being picked off one by one. A friend dies in his arms. By the time Franklin takes up a rifle to engage the enemy sharpshooter, his shipmates are hysterical, screaming at him to hurry up and fire. He does the opposite. He slows down. Bullets ricochet off the wall behind him, but Franklin takes his time. He points the rifle at the rigging and calculates the angles, height, and distance. He wanted to fire only if he was completely sure that he could hit his target. Then he fired. When the sharpshooter tumbles to the deck, the message is clear. Even in war, when everything speeds up to a blur, slowness can prevail. Franklin refuses to rush his shot. He keeps his head, while all around are losing theirs. He triumphs. His slowness is heroic."

~ Sten Nadolny, *The Discovery of Slowness*

Slow Motion training is extremely beneficial for slowing down the mind and the body, so that the sculler understands, feels, and records the accuracy of Movements. A few years ago, I was coaching a young Naval Academy graduate at Craftsbury Sculling Camp. He was having a difficult time grasping the concept of Slow Motion until I spoke of it as the "Tai Chi" of sculling. Immediately, the light bulb went on and he became a convert. So Slow Motion is an excellent exercise for athlete and crew. You can easily self-analyze Slow Movements, which you cannot do at higher speeds. It also gives the coach an opportunity to analyze. His eye can see more of the details of each athlete's timing. "You must be slow on the inside to be fast on the outside and through unhurried, controlled movements, you acquire more self-awareness, concentration, and patience." [92] It also provides an opportunity to adjust the athlete's dynamic posture, if the work is being done on the ergometer. Slow Motion is very effective for drills and simulation exercises.

Claxton, British psychologist delineates between Fast Thinking and Slow Thinking. For Claxton, Fast Thinking is rational, analytical, linear, and logical. This is the type we use under the pressure of racing. [93] Slow Thinking is the type that we require when we are engaged in practicing the stroke. It stirs our imagination, particularly when we are in Slow Motion practice pieces. This is the "wisdom of slowness." Relaxation and

---

[92] Carl Honore, *In Praise of Slowness*, p.130-131
[93] Carl Honore, *In Praise of Slowness*, p.121.

Slow Motion Movement

slowness go hand in hand. Relaxation is the precursor to Slow Thinking. As people think more creatively, we are calm, unhurried and free from stress. A famously counterintuitive piece of advice from Jackie Stewart, the Formula One Champion, "Sometimes to be faster you have to be slower." [94]

Slow Motion inserted into the training program is critical for four reasons:

- One, it provides an opportunity for the athlete to feel Movements and dynamic posture, more accurately;
- Two, it is so important for developing timing of various components;
- Three, it is an excellent form of exercise for doing Quiet Sitting while sitting in the shell. It is a nice counter to the speed of contemporary society; and
- Fourth, the athlete can monitor his own breathing.

This Slow Motion practice is especially effective with young overly aggressive males. All that he wants to do initially in the shell, is to pull hard and to pull fast. Slow Motion training, on the other hand, allows him to gain some experience with the accuracy of each movement at an early stage in his development.

---

[94] Carl Honore, *In Praise of Slowness*, p.134.

The Quantum Sculler

Pilates, Yoga, and Tai Chi are all performed with slow motion movements. This has been the case for centuries with Yoga and Tai Chi. Western sport scientists are now beginning to observe and embrace the concept that exercising more slowly can produce better results. So people are walking more slowly and lifting weights more slowly. We are now promoting that a significant amount of rowing training be done in the slow motion mode.

When we speak of relaxing the sculler, I have found that by relaxing the facial muscles, they go faster. One wrote me this comment, "So last night I hooked up my speed coach in my single and experimented with this. The more relaxed my face was, the quicker the shell went. Interesting ... My initial reaction is that by relaxing my face, my shoulders are less tense and my upper body is quieter, so my blades are then just floating at blade depth." In the 100-meter dash, you can see the same relaxed facial feature in the athletes as they power to the finish line. They are so relaxed in the face that their jaw muscles bounce.

Carl Honore wrote, "The struggle to find and live by one's own rhythm defines what it is to be human." In slowness, and specifically the practice of Slow Motion, we are finding our own rhythm. This is a critical factor when we are learning the five Movements of the Release - finding the correct rhythm for the movement.

Slow Motion Movement

This reason is quite important, as we try to add a meditative component to training. It certainly makes us aware of the Quantum nature of the stroke cycle as we realize how connected the Movements are to each other. It also highlights how things are connected in life. We are all connected.

Slow Motion is a feature that is common ground in a number of sports, including golf, tennis, baseball, and rowing, where athletes practice their respective swing actions at lower stroking rates. The golfer for example always takes a practice swing before he addresses the tee. This form of simulation exercise is employed as a warm-up and precursor to the actual competition. It is almost like a reminder for the athlete of his stroke pattern.

Scott Ford (whom I cited earlier), an excellent Tennis Professional, has this to add to the subject of Slow Motion, "One of the major components of Flow is a sense that everything moves in slow motion. The fact that you are introducing "Slow Motion Training" early on in the learning process, adds this sense of temporal expansion to the mix, right from the get-go. I try to do the same in my tennis training and have found it quite effective when a player is having trouble with some "part" of their stroke. Doing "the whole" stroke in slow motion, even creating contact in slow motion, has an amazing curative effect on the parts of the stroke." He obviously uses this practice with his tennis training and he directly relates Slow Motion to the idea of Flow.

I recall doing high rate short pieces years ago. In the beginning, everything felt rushed and strained. However, after a period of training, everything began to slow down and felt smoother, especially movements of hands and wrists. So mind and body were referencing a much different timing sequence. Everything had slowed down. There was no rush to the movement, when I began doing this practice. Doing Movements in Slow Motion certainly helped this development of a more rhythmic and less rushed action.

Slow Motion is an effective way to perfect the movements as it takes us deep into ourselves. One key practice is simulation exercise on the ergometer of the Recovery from the Release to the Entry without using the handle. This practice uses and emphasizes Trunk Swing. In doing so, we learn the correct action of each movement and subsequent effect on our musculature. All of this is accomplished through our concentrative feelings. It is here that Mind and Matter meet in a slow-moving artistic dance. We are moving deeper into ourselves. We come to look forward to this particular part of the training.

On a personal note, this is how every practice ended for me with a spontaneous slow paddle into the dock. Each ending was done with a specific exercise. I was attempting to perfect the Movements as I completed the practice session. This is where the next day's practice would begin. The shell would slowly come alongside the dock with such accuracy it almost seemed to have a magnet attached to the bow. Many times a bystander would try to assist by catching the inboard scull, but would be waved off so that maneuver could be completed. It was such great fun and a significant source of pride in my skill. I loved this part of the practice, as I could concentrate deeply and feel the exact movement involved with each stroke.

There are other ways to employ Slow Motion as a part of the warm-up or the warm-down. It can also be a way to recover from hard pieces, so that it has regenerative value. It can be an integral part of a long, slow distance piece done in absolute silence. So the exercise is completely meditative.

It cannot be overstated that the training of the athlete must have at its core a strong meditative base. It is imperative that the coach finds ways to insert this training into the program. Slow Motion is one of these ways. It is a meditative practice as much as Quiet Sitting. The same qualities are present, excellent posture, focused breathing, attention to detail, and the utter simplicity of the practice. This is where the coach's flexibility, imagination, and insight must come to the fore. It helps immensely if he is regularly meditating.

This type of training is so important for the expansion of the inner self. This is where the athlete is becoming whole. There are two dimensions to the athlete that have to be ad-

The Quantum Sculler

dressed, the inner and outer athlete. He can make significant strides in his training, preparation, and his racing, if the inner athlete is developed as well as the outer athlete. A significant portion of the athlete's development can come from the use of slow motion sculling and other forms of Quiet Sitting.

Stroke Rating can range from 4 to 16 strokes per minute. At these low rates, it becomes a highly concentrative and exploratory exercise. This development and practice carries over to the sculler's life outside of the shell. He becomes more gentle, more empathetic, and more of a conservationist. "Simple" can be used to describe his life choices. So there is a cultural dimension to this type of training. It is hoped that with fostering of this cultural aspect in the athlete, his performance will be affected positively. He will be more aware, more attentive, and a more sensitive human being. He should begin to feel more connected to the world.

Chapter Fourteen - Continuous Body Movement: Every Part is in Motion.

"The Curlew's wings beat with a strong, rapid, unchanging rhythm, hour after hour. The strokes were deep, smooth, effortless, the wings sweeping low beneath his **belly** at every down stroke and lifting high over the back with each return. Each stroke was an intricate series of gracefully coordinated actions merged with split-second precision into a single, smooth movement. Each portion of the wing had a different flight role to play. It was all reflexive, automatic, and too rapid for conscious control. The Curlew completed three or four wing-beats a second to give him a flight speed of fifty miles an hour.

- From *Last of the Curlews* by Fred Bodsworth

The simple objective for all training is to achieve fluid movement. It encompasses every aspect of training. So we use the term Movement Training, which is an inclusive phrase. It includes training in the shell, work on the ergometer, jumping rope, weight training, winter running and cross country skiing, body weight training, and daily meditative activity. The terminology of "technique" or "style" are too exclusive, much too limiting. Every activity in which we engage must be judged in terms of fluidity and posture. Fluidity and Posture of the body in and out of the shell are paramount. These days, while I coach Vince, my Masters Sculler, I am constantly watching the Movement of his Bow Ball. I want to see it in a continuous, steady movement forward. So we attempt to become a highly flowing instrument of grace and power. The Body is viewed as a complete organism with all parts moving in a continuous fashion. The Trunk Swing with leg action is continuously engaged except for a momentary pause at the Release at the completion of the Drive phase. Arms move continuously as well. Hands never stop, not even with a slightest pause. Any pause in any part of the Total Movement is simply not good physics, except, as stated earlier, where there is a slight pause of the seat at the Release. For this continuous action, the body must be extremely flexible, like that of a dancer. Training the athlete through dance is an ideal strategy. In multiple boats, shoulders of the athletes should all be over the keel line throughout the stroke cycle. Movements of shoulders and heads should be a display of exact and fine coordination. Arms are extended forward at a very slight angle from shoulders at the entry. This positioning keeps the connection between arms, trunk, and legs at this critical point in the Stroke Cycle.

    Yoga has to be an important part of the physical training regimen as well as being essential for mental and spiritual development. With this type of training, proper posture is stressed for

Continuous Body Movement: Every Part is in Motion

strength, core training, and power. Part of the Yoga Posture parallels the Entry position with knees placed under armpits. This allows you to become, as coach Steve Fairbairn expressed it so well, "like a coiled spring."

The teaching method for continuous motion will follow Scott Ford's holistic Parallel Teaching. Four drills will be employed:

- The quarter front-end drill for the Entry;
- The quarter back-end drill for the Release;
- The two pause drill, pausing at three-quarter slide and the hands-position for the Drive Phase; and
- The three pause drill, pausing at the hands-position and at full-slide with blade in the water, rest, returning back to hands-position. This is for the Recovery Phase.

Eventually, drills will be reduced to the three-pause drill only. With this approach, we are grouping more of the movements together, so that there is less instruction to the athlete and more doing on his part. The wholeness of the stroke is emphasized and becomes primary, rather than the parts of the stroke. Detailed coaching of the parts will come later in the coaching process.

I vividly remember the simple, direct strides of Sebastian Coe, Herb Elliott, and the legwork of the great Czech runner

The Quantum Sculler

Emil Zatopek. This morning, I tried to be extra attentive to both to the posture of my meditative sitting position and to my dynamic posture during my morning walk that followed. I follow the principle of stacking the various segments of the body directly on top of one another. It is the same principle of the skyscraper or the giant Redwood trees. It is particularly important at my age to monitor your stride. Your steps must be flexible, erect and light. It is an easy, effortless gait that I am striving for, an effulgence of motion.

These accounts of athleticism, if developed in the sculler, are a precursor for Flow. Every step is a precious moment in time. It is a process of not only deep concentration, but also of deep, deep awareness. We must be attentive to our natural gait in and out of the shell. In the shell, this same lightness is displayed in each stroke as an important quality to our movement. From our meditative sitting position we learn to relax the body and elongate the spine. We sit tall and balance the body. We carry this posture into the shell as well as out of it, when we walk.

Movement cannot be the dictate of ergometer scores or how much weight is lifted. It is the immeasurable fluid, subtle action that determines the right Movements. The Body is a singular vibratory mechanism that is absolutely congruent with the vibrations of the shell. This must be the poetry of our movements and smooth action, our enduring purpose of training.

Continuous Body Movement: Every Part is in Motion

The consciousness and skill development must progress together as a unified process of training. This process is whole, non-fragmented and a deep witness to the Implicate level of Bohm's reality, where everything is connected.

Chapter Fifteen - Level Run of the Shell

Level run of the shell requires that both the body and shell flow with a continuous even movement. Body movements must be smooth and horizontal. This starts with arm action from the extended arm position at the Entry to the flexion of arms at the Release. This transition must be smooth. The action is continuous, fluid and even, with no yanking of the handle near the Release. Arms flow into the Recovery from the Release and Follow-Through, as a unitary action. The movement from the Drive to initial phase of the Recovery should entail a minimum of wrist action. Wrists should not punctuate the end of the Drive. Wrists should remain flat allowing fingers to perform the Release movements.

In multiple shells, all of shoulders, elbows, heads, arms, and legs must be in perfect alignment. This is where simulation exercises, undertaken over the winter months, can be of great assistance. The over-riding principle is that the aligned body must stride with the Run of the shell. Every part of the body is running parallel with the gunwales for most of the stroke. You sit, glide, and drive over the narrow keel line.

The blade should enter the water quickly, moving automatically to blade depth. It remains at blade depth throughout the Drive. You can test the blade depth with an oar on the dock with for your crews watching. If the blade is too deep or too shallow there can be no Bernoulli Effect, and there will not be a depression created behind the blade.

Neat precise blade work is required of all accomplished scullers. Pressure on the handle applied through arms and hands must parallel pressure on the blade. It must be steady and horizontal. Trunk Swing is angled at the Entry in order to obtain length to the Stroke. Movement backward is a steady, level, and subtle transition from extension of the Trunk at the Entry, to a slight extension of the Trunk at the Release. This movement appears to be horizontal. At half-slide the Trunk is perpendicular. From this point to the Release, legs and trunk work together as an integrated unit, finishing together and supporting the slightly trailing arm action. There is a quality of lightness and no strain to drive action. As Swing approaches the bow end of the Slide, the orientation of the Body should be upward. The Sculler sits perfectly erect, yet relaxed, with Trunk leaning slightly in the direction of the bow. The Sculler should perform a quick visualization of his bow deck running constantly and being level without any trace of dipping. At the same time, he watches his stern deck to see that there is no rising of this part of the shell as he completes the Drive Phase of the Stroke.

The most effective drill for the Drive is the Three Pause Drill where you pause with hands three inches off the body after the Release, pause at full-slide, and then pause with blade in the water. Finally, you pull through to the Hands Position.

Recovery action begins with five Movements out of the bow as described in the Recovery section earlier. Steady swing from the hips is crucial for level run of the shell. It is also critical that Swing is tightly married to the seat moving forward. The stern deck should remain level throughout this part of the Stroke. It is important that the sculler observe his stern, watching for any dipping of the deck at the Entry. It helps if the swing from the hips is horizontal and the pendular action is subtle and unnoticeable. This major movement is a precursor for the overall Flow of shell and body. In a further development of the learning process the Trunk Swing becomes a natural glide forward or an instinctual movement.

So, the Stroke looks complete with no loose ends between body, blades and shell. The ingredients are a single unit, a "well-fitted" shoe. It is a "tight" system. Pressure on the foot stretcher is equal on both feet. The same is true for lateral pressure on the sculling oarlocks. These three points of contact, seat, feet, and oarlocks, maintain a stable, balanced platform that is so essential for an effective Entry and Drive. It is important to remain symmetrical to the keel at all points in the Stroke. Seat posture and relationship of the Body to the instrument is similar to the Equestrian and Bicy-

Level Run of the Shell

cle Racer. To maintain this strong position, the abdominal core has to be thoroughly trained.

It is the work of arms over the last six inches of the Drive, while increasing handle speed in a smooth controlled manner that provides the feel of even pressure on the blade face from the entry to the release. Visualizing the bow deck remaining level and sitting up with an even pressure on the blade face are critical elements for keeping the shell level at the end of the Drive. This helps immensely in having a clean Release with the Stroke being rowed through. There is a little added length to each Stroke at the Release with these elements in place. In addition, your vision is split between looking over the stern, at about a three-foot level, and at the same time watching the movement of your stern. These practices help immensely in keeping the shell running level. You have to practice these elements, both at slow-motion and at racing speed.

The overall effect is similar to the movement of Ned Hanlan. The movement of Hanlan's shell was described, "as if pulled by a string." [95] Indeed, Hanlan referred to this quality as the horizontal stroke, and so, there was no porpoise-like action to his shell. The boat slid easily and effortlessly through the water. You must be observant to what is occur-

---

[95] West, J. Thomas. *Ned Hanlan*, p2.

ring to the movement of the shell. You must see and feel the shell running underneath your body mass. You have to be attentive. As a coach, I am constantly monitoring the action of the shell, looking at the stern and looking at bow. I am looking for a level shell with continuous run to it.

Chapter Sixteen - The Flow State

Find your beauty, my heart, from the world's movement, like the boat that has the grace of the wind and the water.
  - Rabindranath Tagore, *Stray Birds*.

The athlete, in achieving a certain level of competency, may begin to think about Flow. The flow state in rowing begins with the attempt to have smooth, whole movements. Flow is the action of moving along in a steady, continuous stream such as the flow of water into a pool. Each part must be performed smoothly, as part of a greater whole. With this type of performing the Whole Movement, you are unable to separate out the parts. For this reason, focus centers on larger more encompassing movements of recovery and drive phases.

Scott Ford, a tennis expert, has identified the ingredients of Flow: "Playing in the zone makes you feel whole because it is wholeness itself – the whole of your unified body-mind in a one-to-one interface with the whole of the athletic environment. The whole you unified with the whole game. That's the zone, and its elegant call is the call of oneness. How do you bring the body-mind and the athletic environment together into a unified whole? The way you bring together the body-mind and the athletic environment into a unified whole is to bring them all into a state of "presence". Presence is the great unifier. It unifies your body and your mind by uniting them in the same spatiotemporal dimension – the present." Scott further elaborates when he writes, "In other words, by fixing your focus on the empty space of your contact zone, you simultaneously defocus from the people, places, and objects to which "self" attaches. Focusing on your contact zone is focusing on nothing, "no-thing." Self is thus attached to nothing. So instead of self relative to the people, places, and objects of form, you have created an experience of self, relative to empty space, self relative to nothing. And self relative to nothing, is "no self", the selfless state in which you are released from the bondage of ego and invited to experience the freedom and fullness of your own true nature." We do this when we concentrate on our mantra outlined below. The concentration is not fixed on the shell, or the oars, or the water. His thinking is fixed on "nothing", so he remains in the present.

The Run of the shell is followed by the development of mental Flow through heightened concentration on timing of the Entry. Mental Flow emerges out of Physical Flow of Shell and Body, which the sculler concentrates so much of his energy and focus to achieve. Then the physical and mental are combined in a simple overall flowing motion that is endless and timeless. However at some point the mental state of the athlete must shift from his concentration on the specific serial parts to the unified parallel mode of operation. The parts become a blur in contrast to the unified whole stroke. He is fixed on "nothing". The sculler fixes his gaze about 3 feet above the end of the stern and the sweep rower focuses about 1 foot in front of the neck of the person in front of him. This fixation on empty space or nothingness, places the sculler in the ever-present "now".

Interface with the water environment occurs at two places in the stroke cycle, the entry and the release. These positions have to remain dynamic. Movements have to be continuous and smooth and the length of the stroke must be maintained. Length at the entry requires that the body is erect and reaching from the hips with the knees under the armpits (anatomical pinpoint). For the release, the trunk is 15 degrees past the perpendicular with the outside hand completing the drive at the outside edge of the abdomen with the hand in the line of pulling (sweep rowing). The hand is positioned at right angles to the handle and not parallel. The parallel positioning of the outside hand leads to a subtle stopping of the action. To foster continuous action, the release and feathering actions are done with both hands, thus no division of labor. You must be in the same place at each transition phase for each stroke. This is what causes Flow to be achieved.

There are four ingredients that must be accomplished during every stroke in order to achieve the magical and mystical

The Quantum Sculler

Flow state. These movements must become part of the natural process and as such, are part of our non-thinking action:

- Smooth action of forearms and elbows (anconeus muscle) out of bow,
- Controlled, well-timed, swing forward,
- Quick, well-placed, entry at blade depth, and
- Even pressure, "pull what you can handle," drive phase.

This state of consistent muscle action must be practiced over and over in these specific phases at slow-motion speed (10 to 14 strokes per minute). At this speed of movement, the mind can be highly concentrated. It is the high concentration of the mind that is able to bring mind and body together. It is a Mindful practice of the two major parts that are seen by the mind to be an integral part of the larger whole Stroke. So eventually, in performing the Stroke, the Mind functions intuitively. Thus, Flow can be produced each time the athlete takes a stroke, especially if the athlete employs the Mind Piece mantra of being long, continuous, smooth, and relaxed. This Flow is a direct result of smooth, consistent length of the muscle action at the key points of the entry and release. Thus, muscle action is integrated with intuitive thinking. A state of Plasticity has occurred in the Mind.

Since the beginning of modern science, the most important breakthrough in understanding the brain, and its relationship to the Mind, is the discovery that the brain has Plasticity. Neuroplasticity is the property of the brain that enables it to change its own structure and function in response to activity and mental experience.

Conscious Rowing (Slow Motion) is certainly a marvelous neuroplasticity exercise, exactly the kind of concentration required to preserve existing neurons in the brain. It is quite similar to the kind of attention that a rock climber must pay to each and every move. It is also similar to how a student of Tai Chi must concentrate his full attention on each joint movement, breath, and muscle contraction.

Plasticity promotes that the mind must be completely connected, in the present, to the body and the environment. There is an intimate wholeness in this approach. Connection and integration is from the smallest cell in the body to the oars, the shell, and the water. A light rhythmic touch should be involved. Nothing is heavy. This is the manner by which the athlete completes all of his activities - sitting and walking with lightness.

To race in this manner, the athlete must be mindful of all his actions. This begins with land warm-ups and carries out onto the water with pre-race warm-up. The warm-up culminates in quiet sitting for a few moments at the starting line. He is mindful and is highly prepared to begin his Flow to the finish line using smooth, well-trained muscle action. As Amy Wettergreen, a William Smith student, once said to me after a race at Syracuse University, "We did not feel any effort, fatigue, or sore muscles, until we entered our cars to return to Geneva." Her crew experienced the same Flow at a championship race in Worcester, Massachusetts.

When you are *In Flow*, it does feel effortlessness. Flow begins with the mental state and the athlete's awareness and understanding of smooth muscle action. It is a presence of both the Mental and the Physical. The athlete then proceeds to practice these smooth movements, the doing part of the equation.

This is how you begin with the novice. However, there is much less detail addressed at this point with the Novice. So, there is also less instruction and more "experiencing" by the young sculler, more "doing and exploring".

In this manner, the sculler, from initial instruction, is performing a larger section of the Stroke, which includes the end of the Recovery to the beginning of the Drive actions. This is referred to as the body or trunk swing. It requires a much higher level of concentration to have everything -- Legs, Blade and Trunk arrive together at Full-Reach. Movement of the Trunk is a critical component to the eventual Flow of the Body.

Premier dance artists of the 20th Century (Gene Kelly, Ginger Rogers, and Fred Astaire) thoroughly understood that they had to make their dance movements look effortless for their audience, even though it took tremendous amounts of practice, en-

The Flow State

ergy and concentration to achieve this fluid state. Kelly said, "At this point, Dance became Art." The same is true for sculling. It becomes a dance and a form of art. Any art form of movement must be made to look easy and fluid to the observer. It is not a struggle to apply, and to continue to apply, power. It is not a heavy movement of strength being applied. It is light and dance-like. However, it is actually very intensive, requiring enormous amounts of practice, accuracy, and patience. At the same time, the performer's will and mind are undergoing a positive change.

The sculler concentrates on observing the continuous run of the stern. The continuous level run of the stern is an excellent indicator of the bow running level and continuously. This continuous Run of the shell is dependent upon precise timing of body swing with blade entry. Run is the physical flow of the shell. It is incumbent on the coach to watch how the bow of the shell is moving. He also must develop an analytical eye for each and every part of the stroke cycle. When you achieve this intricate timing, the shell responds immediately, each time that you take a stroke. You can feel it. This feeling of immediate-applied power invigorates the mental component. It is such a fluid and simple action. The controlled, well-timed, swing forward and backward is the real "trigger" for Flow. This involves a highly concentrated mental effort on the smooth execution of the movements. This is exactly what I experienced a few times on the Port Dalhousie course in St. Catharines many years ago. To this day, I have not forgotten the feeling of the lightness of these actions.

George Pocock said, "Do I make myself clear about the timing that is involved in rowing? It is pretty elementary, but suppose the eight men in a boat were eight golfers at a tee. Line them up, one behind the other, and make them bring their clubs up to exactly the same height, swing and hit the ball with the sound of one crack. Eight men hitting that golf ball with one crack — that is what a crew has to do, when it hits the water. You've got to hit with one crack or the boat will not respond." [96]

Flow becomes a form of higher consciousness, where physical timing is exquisite and correct power is applied. Everything has a quality of smoothness, lightness, and unhurried exactness. It is a state where body, blade, and shell are perfectly timed. Nothing is strained. Consciousness of the individual creates this. The beauty of sculling at this point is so striking. It is utter perfection.

With the sculler's entry, everything is in a state of change, Body, shell, action of blade, and the water. But there is an underlying unity between the whole body, shell, and blade in the water. There is no preparation of blade for entry, only a contin-

---

[96] George Newell, *Ready All: George Yeoman Pocock and Crew Racing*, p.85.

uous flow. It is a part of a whole movement. This method for the entry movement requires quickness and fine athleticism by the athlete. This quickness of movement becomes one of the traits that the sculler must cultivate in his training, much like endurance, speed, and strength. However, this quickness has no hint of being rushed. This, I feel, is what conventional people are missing in training of the athlete - the ability to move quickly under control. In this specific case, it is relaxed fingers, hands, and wrists that have to move quickly, with subtlety, and deftness. Relaxed fingers allow the handle to pivot smoothly at each end of the Slide as transitions take place. This is where Slow Motion Sculling plays such an important role for the athlete to learn to move accurately and under control. He learns to move slowly so that he can move fast. There is no waste to his movements. The entry movements become a major part of his subtle consciousness and the Implicate Order. This is in stark contrast to the exaggerated movements of conventional sculling, where body angle is set out of bow and the athlete prepares for the Entry.

    The sculler feels the Shell run as a continuous, sliding movement, with arms moving in and out in a fluid, direct fashion from the elbows. The objective is seeing the visual effect as being upwards.

    The focus of Consciousness must be in the moment and on the whole. It cannot be mechanical. There has to be a flow to the thought connected to the movement of the body. The Flow state can also be manufactured at will with the concentration on the Mind Pieces (See below). In the sweep shell, this level of consciousness must permeate the thought and actions of all oarsmen as well as the coxswain. They must form a tight, bonded, connected unit.

The leg actions of two great runners, Herb Elliott and Sebastian Coe, with continuous and beautiful fluidity, are comparable to the continuous action of the arms in sculling. In both cases, these actions are the foundation for the Flow State. The arm action is simple, horizontal and direct. It helps immensely, if you round the movement at the Release through light touch of fingers on the handle. The motion is continuous and uninterrupted. Action at the Release is helped with a minimum of wrist action. The primary impetus for arm action comes from the elbows moving into and out from the Body.

However, the mind and body have to be connected to the underlying thought, the consciousness. This is the energy field that surrounds us. It is the shell, oars, body, and the water. You are part of the Implicate Order, when your thinking goes in this direction. You are part of a whole and you are not fragmented with Mind doing one thing and matter and body, doing another. Everything is inter-connected, as a part of the Implicate order. It is so effortless and involves so much delicate feel with

The Flow State

fingers, arms, trunk, and legs. Nothing is heavy. The total movement feels light.

In sculling, we must be symmetrical with equal pressure on the footplates, and on both sides of our butts. Alignment of the Body involves side-to-side, up-and-down, and forward-and-back positions of our torso. Establishing this balanced sitting position, permits the body to relax. Our leg placement at the Entry is symmetrical to the keel line with the knees under the armpits. Our light finger grasp of both hands on the oar handles is also equal. Hands should be level at each end of the Slide. This symmetry must also be the case for sweep boats. We have in recent years tended to move away from this practice in the sweep boats. The reach of arms must be predominately a forward action rather than a side action. So the rigging of the shell must reflect this symmetrical situation for each athlete. All of this attention to the details promotes the development of flow.

Philosopher Satish Kumar has this view - Life is a journey of discovery. Certainty is only possible when there is something fixed and permanent, whereas reality is constantly moving and changing. It is constantly undergoing a transformation. If our minds are tethered to a fixed belief, a certain knowledge, then how can we cope with this constant change? Since reality is not static, we need swift minds and pliable hearts. Only then, can we be responsive to the dynamic nature of existence.

The Quantum Sculler

Mentally, the sculler should feel completely coordinated and should begin to feel energy coming from his immediate surroundings, oars, shell, body, and the water. It is important that we tap into the energy from the water. This is our intimate environment that changes from day to day. We learn to flow with the conditions and the specific wave action on any particular day. This is where the sculler's flow begins, as he starts to connect with the quantum energy system. He is now a fully-engaged child of the natural environment. His consciousness has shifted to a more universal mode of awareness and operation. He experiences pure delight and wonder, as his shell slides along effortlessly. There is not enough river to contain his enthusiastic efforts.

A strategy for when pain and fatigue set in, is to employ "Mind Pieces", where you concentrate on the mantra of "long, continuous, smooth, and relaxed". This usually starts to occur during the Drive, when the Stroke seems heavy and labored. So this is a strategy and mantra that I formulated to combat fatigue and pain. It allows the athlete to finish the race with strength and ease. Lindsey Hochman's experience with Mind Pieces follows, "I shared the mind pieces with Steve, and told him about what I experienced. I thought that was an awesome exercise and felt as though I was the closest to Flow as I have ever been. On Sunday, I agreed to do a 15-mile run with one of my friends here who used to be an elite marathon runner. Around mile twelve, when I was starting to hurt, I remembered the Mind Pieces and started thinking - stay continuous, long, smooth, and relaxed. It was AMAZING! For the last three miles I felt like a gazelle, and completely disconnected myself from my sore muscles and relaxed into the run. It was the best I have ever felt. Very cool!"

Lindsey was experiencing the Flow phenomena. These Mind Pieces put the person into a very different mental space. You are much more relaxed as your mind shifts from focusing on pain and fatigue, to concentrating on length of your movements, to continuous nature of the movements, to the smooth action you are feeling, with everything connected to a relaxed state of being. It is an exhilarating feeling of pure joy. This mantra can become a mantra for activating the Flow phenomenon as the athlete goes internal into the deeper recesses of his mind. There is a shift from thinking about the parts to thinking about the whole body movement as it interfaces with the environment.

"When working 90%, the athlete is able to be much more integrated with the shell and is able to listen, feel, and observe his surroundings like he had never could do at the 100% level. The 90% level allows the muscles to fire at a level that is very efficient. He is not over-powering as per usual, so the whole muscle, and the mind-intensity thing was not blurred-out. Backing off slightly, the mind opens up and observes. As long as the 90% rule is not violated, the athlete is able to actually observe himself

The Quantum Sculler

from the outside and then make corrections from an observer standpoint."

This awareness is assisted in part by working where it feels that he is only pulling with 90% effort. This level of pulling erases all anxiety and tension from the body. This law is a principle from the former track coach, the late Bud Winter. This rule helps immeasurably in eliminating all anxiety.

David Bohm recognized that separate objects, entities, structures, and events in the visible or Explicate World around us are relatively autonomous, stable, and temporary "sub totalities" derived from a deeper, Implicate Order of unbroken wholeness. Bohm employed the analogy of a flowing stream, "On this stream, one may see an ever-changing pattern of vortices, ripples, waves, splashes, etc., which evidently have no independent existence as such. Rather, they are abstracted from the flowing movement, arising and vanishing in the total process of the flow. Such transitory subsistence, as may be possessed by these abstracted forms, implies only a relative independence or autonomy of behavior, rather than absolutely independent existence as ultimate substances. We must learn to view everything as part of an Undivided Wholeness in Flowing Movement". Bohm is suggesting that the whole universe can be thought of as a kind of giant, flowing hologram, or "holo-movement", in which a total order is contained, in some implicit sense, in each region of space and time.

The Flow State

De-focusing, as mentioned at the outset of this chapter, is counterintuitive. By controlling the focus of the eye you control the focus of the mind. In flow you are focusing on the total environment and this will not occur if you are focused on any one point. Again, it is important to keep the flow of the movement going at each end of the stroke- the sculler's entry and the two handed release with the sweep people.

The level run of the shell requires that both the body and shell flow with a continuous even movement. Body movements must be smooth and horizontal. . Arms flow into the Recovery from the Release and into the follow-through, as a unitary action. The movement from the Drive to initial phase of the Recovery should entail a minimum of wrist action. Wrists should not punctuate the end of the drive. Wrists should remain flat allowing fingers to perform the release movements.

In multiple shells, all of shoulders, elbows, heads, arms, and legs must be in perfect alignment. This is where simulation exercises, undertaken over the winter months, can be of great assistance. The over-riding principle is that the aligned body must stride with the Run of the shell. Every part of the body is running parallel with the gunwales for most of the stroke. You sit, glide, and drive over the narrow keel line.

Neat precise blade work is required of all accomplished scullers. Pressure on the handle applied through arms and hands must parallel pressure on the blade. It must be steady

The Quantum Sculler

and horizontal. Trunk Swing is angled at the Entry in order to obtain length to the Stroke. Movement backward is a steady, level, and subtle transition from extension of the Trunk at the Entry, to a slight extension of the Trunk at the Release. This movement appears to be horizontal. At half-slide the Trunk is perpendicular. From this point to the Release, legs and trunk work together as an integrated unit, finishing together and supporting the slightly trailing arm action. There is a quality of lightness and no strain to drive action. As Swing approaches the bow end of the Slide, the orientation of the Body should be upward. The Sculler sits perfectly erect, yet relaxed, with Trunk leaning slightly in the direction of the bow. The Sculler should perform a quick visualization of his bow deck running constantly and being level without any trace of dipping. At the same time, he watches his stern deck to see that there is no rising of this part of the shell as he completes the Drive Phase of the Stroke.

    The most effective drill for the Drive is the Three Pause Drill where you pause with hands three inches off the body after the Release, pause at full-slide, and then pause with blade in the water. Finally, you pull through to the Hands Position.

    The stern deck should remain level throughout this part of the Stroke. It is important that the sculler observe his stern, watching for any dipping of the deck at the Entry. It helps if the swing from the hips is horizontal and the pendular action is subtle and unnoticeable. This major movement is a precursor for the overall Flow of shell and body. In a further development of the learning process the Trunk Swing becomes a natural glide forward or an instinctual movement.

Therefore, the Stroke looks complete with no loose ends between body, blades and shell. The ingredients are a single unit, a "well-fitted" shoe. It is a "tight" system. Pressure on the foot stretcher is equal on both feet. The same is true for lateral pressure on the sculling oarlocks. These three points of contact, seat, feet, and oarlocks, maintain a stable, balanced platform that is so essential for an effective Entry and Drive. It is important to remain symmetrical to the keel at all points in the Stroke. Seat posture and relationship of the Body to the instrument is similar to the equestrian and bicycle racer. To maintain this strong position, the abdominal core has to be thoroughly trained.

I recall watching a practice of Bob Janousek's British eight in 1976 before the Montreal Olympics. The shell simply slid through the water with each stroke. The gunwales were level and in continual horizontal motion. It was so beautiful to watch. The crew ended up coming second to the East Germans. It was a similar movement to Hanlan's single described as being pulled by a string.[97] Indeed, Hanlan re-

---

[97] West, J. Thomas. *Ned Hanlan*, p 2.

ferred to this quality as the horizontal stroke, and so, there was no porpoise-like action to his shell. The boat slid easily and effortlessly through the water.

It is the arms that do the work over the last six inches of the Drive. Handle speed increases in a smooth controlled manner that provides the feel of even pressure on the blade face from the entry to the release. Visualizing the bow deck remaining level and sitting up with an even pressure on the blade face are critical elements for keeping the shell level at the end of the Drive. This helps immensely in having a clean Release with the Stroke being rowed through. There is a little added length to each Stroke at the Release with these elements in place. In addition, your vision is split between looking over the stern, at about a three-foot level, and at the same time watching the movement of your stern. These practices help immensely in keeping the shell running level. You have to practice these elements, both at slow-motion and at racing speed.

You must be observant to what is occurring to the movement of the shell. You must see and feel the shell running underneath your body mass. You have to be attentive. As a coach, I am constantly monitoring the action of the shell, looking at the stern and looking at bow. I am looking for a level shell with continuous run to it.

The Flow State

In performing the Stroke Cycle, we do have to recognize that everything is in flux. It is part of the larger life journey that engages us. Nothing is static except for the slight pause of Trunk and Legs at the Release. The Sculler becomes a master of perpetual motion and change.

Chapter Seventeen - Sculling as an Art Form

Poetic motion

Finer rowing and sculling require all parts to be balanced, aligned, precise, well-timed, outside and inside, with every muscle and nerve cell functioning communally. One's head, shoulder, arm, elbow, leg, and knee are aligned. Segments are form. The Sculler practices patience and Mindful concentration. Flow of the whole Movements is achieved through drilling, repetition, and centered concentration. Sculler and Shell flow like a gentle stream. The Recovery integrates very exactly the Seat and Trunk movements. The Drive totally combines Trunk, Legs, and Arms from the Entry to the Release.

These movements provide Flow to Body and Shell. There is no setting or preparation for the next Movement. Every body part displays continuous motion. The motion is Implicate, so subtle, and simple, with little separation between the part and the whole. It is exquisite! Finally, hands and fingers engage with very high relaxation and ever so light touch. We are witnessing high Art, similar to ice dancing or skiing in deep snow. The effect is powerful.

Sculling as an Art Form

The Shell runs swift. Flowing swiftness foregrounds the vivid natural world enveloping the shell, river, trees, bank, and foliage, a complete picture. The sculler and his efficient movements form an intimate relationship with this backdrop. Precision Flow Movement and tight community are at play. This is Poetic Motion.

- Jimmy Joy

One dimension of sculling that has not been explored is sculling as an art form with the coach as an artist or choreographer. This is natural extension of the development of the sculler's skills and consciousness. This is the primary reason behind our taking up the sport and its skills not a focus on actual winning. It is the personal development involved that that motivates and spurs us on. For this, you need a sculling master, a mentor steeped in the art of the sport. A person who knows all the nuances associated with skill development. This is the point where consciousness and skill converge and form unity of mind and body.

For George Pocock, "the movements had to be demonstrated with constant practice until the oarsman gets the true 'feel' for the boat. It literally has to become part of him. It is a living thing, and like a spirited horse, it will work well for him if it is handled right. Just as a skilled rider is said to become like part of his horse, the skilled oarsman must become a part of boat."

As protected humans who have lost much of our sensory keenness, we are at a great disadvantage. We need to reconnect with the natural world and remove ourselves from the electronic world that functions as a parallel universe. This is how the students show up for rowing in colleges. They have lost the connection to their bodies and the natural world around them. To connect with the world of the senses we need to run outside away from the indoor machines. We must learn to feel our body as it travels through space, *balancing on a thin strip of wood.* Any weight training should be done as much as possible with free weights. We need some exposure to dancing, yoga, and bodyweight exercises done slowly. We need to take a piece of rope and do rope jumping. Gone are the days when a youngster came to the sport having worked with their hands during the summer months. To learn how to work wisely and really feel the Movements, we need these body activities that are separated from the machines. We need to learn to feel our whole body and how it moves effectively. The young sculler learns the mechanics. He needs to learn through the relaxed hold of the handles, the feel of the relaxed body, the feel of the blade taking, holding, and releasing the water, and the feel of the shell moving continuously and smoothly through the water.

It is almost like we are seeking a Native knowledge. "Native people are still living in subsistence patterns. They possess a sophisticated and necessary knowledge of place that is absolutely beyond most of us today. Their brains are trained in the most natural ways possible. Their values and knowledge are bedrock for understanding things like bird language. So, native knowledge and scientific knowledge are two ways of paying close attention to nature around us. Native knowledge is scientific knowledge without the trappings." The modern coach, unlike the old Thames watermen and scullers, is still preoccupied with his speed coach. This is the "scientific" approach, but it completely eliminates any natural understanding and feeling for your subject matter. For effective coaching we need the balance between both approaches.

On the other hand, the native knowledge way is where connections are made between sculling skills and the natural world. This is where a relationship develops between the sculler and the coach. This is where eventually the coach becomes the student, the lifelong student of the movements operating in nature. This is the path that Percy Cerutty, George Pocock, Bert Haines and Harry Parker took in their lifetimes and now, Tom Terharr and Paul Thompson are doing the same with their lives and with their crews. The coach's athlete develops to the level where he has the pertinent information and the coach must ask him about what is happening. They are both on a quest for excellence. It is partially a spiritual/meditative quest and partially a quest for finer movements to occur. But, encompassing this enterprise is the quality of Wholeness where everything is related and where everything is connected.

Our modern science is reductionist, mechanistic, and objective. There is no feeling or beauty involved. No learning from the elements is involved in this approach to our sport. There is no room for the water, the shell or our own bodies as teachers. Likewise there is no room for a poet such as George Pocock. But, you still need to see the relationships between body segments and seek to connect these segments to the whole movement and to the movement of the shell. You have to join, rather than divide or fragment. The old Thames watermen, working long hours on the river learned how to conserve, as well as produce energy. He learned how to make his movements whole. From our understanding of Bert Haines at Harvard and George Pocock at Washington, they never lost their knowledge and skill of how to move boats. This is the indigenous path in our learning from our forefathers, the Thames watermen. We must return to this path to be the complete sculler. Thus, the compelling need for small boat intensive training. As it turns out, Quantum physics is closer to the indigenous pathway, than to earlier Newtonian physics. In the indigenous ways of knowing, we understand a thing only when we understand it with all four aspects of being -- mind, body, emotion, and spirit. The Western scientist uses only one or two of those ways of knowing -- mind and body. We must return to the world of feelings, touching, sensing, and listening. Simply put, we have to be more sensitive of the whole of the world around us.

In a recent email from Vince Reynolds he asks, "We have to wonder how does one even begin to convey these concepts in the world in which we live today?" I have given this much thought, and even meditated on it, and have come up with the following plans. First, the coach has to have a daily meditation session for 10 - 15 minutes per day. It is an integral part of his training plan. It is done throughout the year both on land and in the shell. The coach has to sit with the athletes when the session is done on land. He should relate the sitting aspect to the sitting done by the indigenous peoples. It is a simple way to touch and relate to the Earth. Secondly, the feeling for the body and how it moves in the shell has to be emphasized. The athlete has to become acutely aware of his body movements and his immediate environment. This is especially true for the city boy, both in and out of the shell.

> We are thankful to our Mother the Earth, for she gives us everything that we need for life. She supports our feet as we walk about upon her. It gives us joy that she still continues to care for us, just as she has from the begin-

ning of time. To our Mother, we send thanksgiving, love, and respect. Now our minds are one.

With this daily Onondaga invocation, what then happens to nationalism, to political boundaries, when allegiance lies with winds and waters that know no boundaries that cannot be bought or sold. We must return to a study of these people who were able to see the wholeness in life. Our daily practice of quiet sitting is an excellent way to expand the minds of the athletes, improve their concentration and provide a different perspective.

There are the two methods of training, the competitive model, and the artistic. The competitive model is an outward form and when unnecessarily stressed develops a polarity between the outward and the inward. We have to strive to bring these two dimensions of the inward and outward together so that there is unity of effort. "When the two energies come together, there is an added quality, the whole being more than the sum of its parts." The competitive method is fragmented, trying much too hard, while the artistic method is whole, balanced and more effective in the long run of things. The competitive pits people against one another rather than striving to have each individual develop to his fullest measure of himself. This is a direction that I feel we are missing when we have people engaged in sport for purely the goal of winning. Enjoyment is missing as well as the pursuit of sport as art. Today, we are too reductionist

Sculling as an Art Form

with our pursuit of numbers. We can't see for example that the ergometer can be used for something other than tests and physical training. So as coaches, we must explore this purpose of sculling as an art form and become better artists/choreographers. We must inspire our students to aspire to reach higher levels of refined movements and consciousness.

> When an archer is shooting for nothing,
> He has all his skill.
> If he shoots for a brass buckle,
> He is already nervous.
> If he shoots for a prize of gold,
> He goes blind
> Or he sees two targets –
> He is out of his mind!
> His skill has not changed. But the prize
> Divides him. He cares.
> He thinks more of winning
> Than of shooting –
> And the need to win
> Drains him of power."
>   - Chuang Tzu

The Quantum Sculler

The artistic method is also more likely to lead to the Flow state where *effort is effortless*. We fully experience enjoyment in our practice. This method does produce efficient movements, especially if each athlete is closely monitored. We simply can scull and scull as an ongoing form of art. It captures our mind as a presence and our total being as a feeling experience. This unified being is something that I feel as a coach and strive to have the athletes feel, as well. It goes well beyond the daily training prescriptions. It goes to our marrow.

Possibly, the one exception of "coach viewed as artist" was George Pocock in Seattle. He conducted his life, his boat building and his coaching as an artist. His everyday practice was one of deep spirituality that had developed naturally from the evolution of his sculling skills and consciousness. Ironically, the artistic approach to the sport can also be quite powerful in its impact on the eventual speed of the shell.

With proper direction from a knowledgeable coach, this philosophy can be a prime motivator for the young sculler. I was fortunate to find such a coach in Robert Fitzpatrick. He was devoted to the sport and to having his athletes scull the shell smoothly and flawlessly. Sculling, under the watchful eye of Fitzpatrick, became a form of art. There was no movement left unchecked with the Old Coach. He expected that each movement would be perfected before moving to the next one. This was mastery training and it was very effective. His coaching practice entailed meticulous attention to details of the many movements of the stroke cycle. My initial exposure to his coaching occurred when I was fifteen years of age, new to the sport, and was fortunate to witness the perfection of Bob's double sculls of the Murphy Brothers in training.

We can witness this exquisite composition in the natural world with the playful dance of a flock of water Swallows or the deliberate flight patterns of the Canadian Geese floating across the majesty of an autumn sky. We are connecting sculling to birds in flight. We are connecting to the natural world. This is where relationships develop between sculler and coach. They are both on a quest for excellence. It is in part a spiritual/meditative quest and partially a movement quest. In multiple boats the key ingredient for this flow, this community of effort is uniform movement of head and shoulders of the group up-and-down the Slide. If anyone is misaligned or out-of-phase, it shows immediately and perpetually. I witnessed this recently while viewing racing at the Royal Henley Regatta in UK. The better crews were more perfectly aligned.

Encompassing this sculling enterprise, is the quality of wholeness. The movements have to be whole and in a constant state of flux. Nothing is static. Fitzpatrick knew this intuitively. In the world of physics, we can become deeply imbedded in David Bohm's Implicate Order, where everything is related and where everything is connected.

The Quantum Sculler

I have seen recently seen two conflicting signs. One displayed in a store front window in our little town, "We are all connected," and the second one, on the tail-end of a Jeep that stated over an American flag, "There is only the one." The former is much more expansive and more in line with the quantum world of connections and relationships. Bohm recognized this dimension in his study and expressed it in the social applications of quantum theory.

We are more likely to reach the Flow State when *effort is effortless*. We fully experience enjoyment in our practice. We can simply and repeatedly scull, as an ongoing form of art. Flow captures our mind as a presence and our total being as a feeling experience. It has both outer and inner dimensions that come to together, at some point, to form a unity.

This is a direction that I feel we are missing, when we are preoccupied with winning. It impedes the development of the artistic. The enjoyment of sculling is missing as well as the pursuit of sport as art. The sport of rowing, as an art form, is a far larger canvas that we trying to work with. It engages both our inner and outer selves. Winter simulation exercises on the ergometer are an excellent means to achieve exactness in individual movements and uniformity in group dynamics which lead to flow in the shell.

It is critical that the athlete maintains his focus on the process. This is precisely described by Eugen Herrigel, in his beautiful little book, *Zen in the Art of Archery*. In archery training, the improperly trained athlete focuses solely on the result - hitting the target. He loses sight of the important goal of learning to shoot correctly. By focusing on the result, he overlooks the real target that is himself.

My feeling is that we should do more as coaches to promote the art of sculling. With this comes the knowledge of detail and wholeness of Movements. It is both a physical and spiritual quest. This personal development involves challenges and spurs us on. For this you need a sculling master, a mentor steeped in the art of the sport, a person who knows all the nuances associated with skill development. This is the point where consciousness and skill converge and form the unity of mind and body.

It is important that the coach set aside a small amount of time during each practice session to view the boat he is coaching as an art form. As well as his role of being an artist, as he attempts to sculpt the movements of the crew.

Therefore as coaches, we must explore this purpose of achieving a dimensional art with rowing and become better artists and choreographers. In achieving this dimension, we must inspire our students to aspire to reach higher levels of refined movements and consciousness. Then, like George Pocock, we become artists.

Chapter Eighteen - Summary

"This life of yours, which you are living is not merely a piece of this entire existence, but in a certain sense, the whole; only this whole is not so constituted that it can be surveyed in one single glance. This, as we know, is what the Brahmins (wise men or priests in the Vedic tradition) express in that sacred, mystic formula, which is yet really so simple and so clear; tat tvam asi, this is you. Or again, in such words as "I am in the east and the west, I am above and below, I am this entire world."

- Erwin Schrodinger wrote this in his book
Meine Weltansicht.

20th century physicists, Nels Bohr, Werner Heisenberg and Erwin Schrödinger regularly read Vedic texts. Heisenberg stated, "Quantum Theory will not look ridiculous to people who have read Vedanta. Vedanta is the conclusion of Vedic thought." These eastern texts see reality as one of Wholeness, as does Quantum Mechanics.

Schrödinger, in speaking about Heisenberg, said, "I had several discussions with Heisenberg. I lived in England then (circa 1972), and I visited him several times in Munich and showed him the whole manuscript chapter by chapter. He was

Summary

very interested and very open, and he told me something that I think is not known publicly because he never published it. He said that he was well aware of these parallels. While he was working on Quantum Theory, he went to India to lecture and was a guest of Tagore. He talked a lot with Tagore about Indian philosophy. Heisenberg told me that these talks had helped him a lot with his work in physics, because they showed him that all these new ideas in Quantum Physics were, in fact, not all that crazy. He realized there was, in fact, a whole culture that subscribed to very similar ideas. Heisenberg said that this was a great help for him." [98]

Precision sculling promotes wholeness and the idea that we take energy from our environment. It is "free energy". "In relating the concepts to life, David Bohm feels that it is Wholeness that goes a long way to bringing together separate nations, different religions, political organizations, economic and racial groups. Fragmentation is the response of this Whole to man's action, guided by Illusory Perception, which is shaped by Separated Thinking." [99]

As coaches, we are engaged in trying to modify athlete's technique and athlete's physical state. What are we trying to do with his mental state? Are we trying to produce or at least en-

---
[98] David Storoy, *Did the Vedic Philosophy Influence the Concept of Free Energy and Quantum Mechanics?*
[99] David Bohm, *Wholeness and the Implicate Order*, p.9.

courage the development of a beautiful mind. This is a mind that has balance, control, discipline, fairness, empathy, and a strong sense of justice. Stillness, Silence and Slowness are the components of training that can substantially affect the mind's development. Here is where sculling and sport can have direct influence on athlete's mental progress. In any coach's mind, this should be a critical objective for training the athlete's mind. When we change the way we practice our sport, we change our minds, we change society, we change our values.

We can look at competition as a measuring stick of our own personal development. It is not a shallow opportunity to achieve power over an opponent, but, a chance to be the very best we can be and to play against our own potential.

Morehei Oshiba, "O'Sensei", the founder of Aikido, is fondly known for his approach towards participants in a contest, by exhorting practitioners to protect the opponent and blend with them. In other words, to see the world through their eyes, is a more cultivated and civilized approach to life. [100]

This is the development of Empathy, referred to above. It is Wholeness, rather than Fragmentation, that must be stressed in the shell and out of it. Fragmentation in any part of the Stroke Cycle vitiates any attempt to achieve Flow. Bohm sees the "unbroken wholeness of the totality of existence as an undivided

---

[100] Correspondence from Barry Robbins

flowing movement without borders. It is possible to comprehend both Cosmos and Consciousness as a single unbroken totality of movement." Both Mysticism and Bohm's Quantum Physics see the world as interconnected. For the sculler, it starts with his Consciousness level in the shell. Is he aware of the interconnectivity of what he is doing? Or does he approach the skill in a fragmented manner? If his approach is the former, then he immediately recognizes how he is connected to his coaches and teammates, then to his family, to his friends, to his community, to his country, and finally to the world and the universe.

This thinking, the Implicate Order from Bohm, can be directly related to the Trunk Swing of Fitzpatrick or Hanlan's Pendular Swing. It is an all-encompassing movement engaging the two major segments of the Stroke Cycle, the Recovery and the Drive. Awareness and thinking in this manner expands our Consciousness that is so necessary for the achievement of the Flow State.

The development of Consciousness must proceed with the progressive improvement of the athlete's skill. As I wrote in *The Mind's Eye*, a few years ago, they go hand in hand. It is all part of a unified approach to coaching and training. It is seamless and natural. The athlete moves effortlessly from Quiet Sitting on land and in the shell, to technical drills for Skill Training. Both practices become ingrained in his daily routine. In laying out the exposition of the various Movements, I have tried to be as detailed as possible. This was done for the sake of absolute clarity.

I am reminded of the teaching of the great Australian Track Coach, Percy Cerutty. The manner, in which, he would observe the fluid motions of small children, animals and dancers. Personally, I see this in my new granddaughter Bea. She is continually in motion, from her books, to the front window to view the buses that arrive for school, to the dining table, and back to her books. Children are constantly in motion. Animals have the same fluid elastic movement in their bodies. The dancer is the epitome of graceful power. The 19th Century artist Edgar Degas was intrigued with movements of dancers and racehorses and made them subjects for his art work, sculptures and paintings.

The athlete has to be totally conscious of his actions. This concentration is necessary, both in and out of the shell. My Masters Sculler Vince Reynolds is applying these principles to his small business of twenty-five people. He recently reported, "I have got to tell you about what it was like here in the shop this past Friday and Saturday. I have never ever in my life had these feelings and experienced anything like it. I am still absolutely thunderstruck by the collective consciousness that was and did occur. It was plain and simple, and it allowed us to make the move to achieve what we did."

Summary

Scott Ford applies this approach to tennis with his unique practices. David Meggyesy is working with the Concepts in his own sculling and his larger work with the eminent American author Jean Houston, who is involved in the "human potential movement". It is a commitment to greater and greater refinement of Mind and Body and the Specific Movements. It is also a commitment to being creative with moving the body and creativity with our consciousness. This must be the standard practice.

David Bohm offers a comment on the connection between the mind and body. "It seems to me that just as the health of the body demands that we breathe properly, so, whether we like it or not, the health of the mind requires that we be creative. That is to say, the mind is not the sort of thing that can properly act mechanically. And this is why we fail, whenever we try to be mechanical." [101]

The Stroke Cycle itself is in a continuous state of flux and creativity. It is an art form when executed properly. It is a culture of awareness, deep implications, and concentrated focus. So the sculler must have a creative mind. It is a wonderful and beautiful thing to witness when the execution is perfected. The Stroke is finely woven and none of his Movements are mechanistic. The process is one of discovery of self, your skill level,

---

[101] David Bohm, *On Creativity*, p.29.

knowledge of the Shell, how it runs, and the vagaries of water. All of this requires that we are creative. Then flexibility in thought process and in body movements are paramount. Each relies on proprioception. In both cases, it is a matter of having a strong involvement and awareness of our feelings.

Writing cogently on man's greater Wholeness, David Bohm states, "Wholeness is what is real and Fragmentation is the response of the Whole to man's action, guided by Illusory Perception, which is shaped by Fragmentary Thought. This new form of insight can best be called Individual Wholeness in Flowing Movement. In this Flow, Mind and Matter are not separate substances. Rather, they are different aspects of one whole and unbroken Movement. True unity in the individual and between man and nature, as well as, between man and man, can only arise in a form of action that does not attempt to fragment the whole of reality." [102]

Using and thinking the whole of Movement involves simplicity and conservation in motions. The Movements become easier and you use less energy to do more, *"Multum in Parvo' - Much in Little."* [103]

Intensity of pursuit of concentration, for both athlete and coach, produces a special relationship between the two. It can

---

[102] David Bohm, *Wholeness and the Implicate Order* p. 9-20.
[103] Wendell Berry, *Harlan Hubbard*, p.29

Summary

best be described as friendship. It is an unconditional acceptance of each other and could well be a model for any coach's relationship with an athlete. Satish Kumar, a wise thinker and teacher, has this to add to the conversation on friendship, "The word for friendship in Buddhism is Metta, and one of the names of Gautama the Buddha is Maitreya. He is not a guru, a master, a prophet, or a divine being. He is simply a friend - Maitreya." [104] So the coach, with a similar concentrative pursuit of excellence that he shares with the student, is simply a friend. This is the unbreakable bond. It is something that I cherish from my experiences in the distant past with the Old Coach.

Consciousness can be advanced by gaining some familiarity with how our brain functions. Fifty years ago the new study area for coaches became physiology. Now I am suggesting that we move in our studies to evolutionary science, neuroscience and the plasticity of the brain. "The body of knowledge and understanding, and the panoply of techniques that go under the name of 'neuroscience' are some of the greatest intellectual achievements of mankind." [105] The work of Norman Doidge, M.D., has been extremely helpful with his references to the great Movement expert, Moshe Feldenkrais, and his extensive passages on plasticity of the brain. It is further evidence that we can

---

[104] Satish Kumar, *Spiritual Compass: The Three Qualities of Life*, p.116.
[105] Raymond Tallis, *Aping Mankind: Neuromania, Darwinitis and the Misrepresentation of Humanity*, p.13.

make significant changes in our brain and bodily movements. He points out the importance of ears and that ears developed first in humans before our brains.

According to Doidge, the ear is related to the higher level of listening above hearing and to good posture and muscle tone throughout the whole body. All of this information is pertinent and can be applied to our coaching. It is information that works from the standpoint of the Whole, mystifying those that persist in localizing the information that is conveyed to athletes.

When you attempt to think and perceive as a whole, it is a significantly different feeling that you are experiencing. This is because our education has stressed the fragmentary so much. It is a wonderful creative art where one finds oneself. Through his fluid motion and the study of the process, the sculler and the coach are creating beautiful minds. This beautiful mind becomes the true objective for our sport practice, where one experiences the beauty and wholeness of the flowing body and the fluid running of the shell. The sculler discovers the magic of bringing these two components together, the skill of the movement and the deep consciousness involved. It is a process of growth in complexity through our skills training and through the expansion of our consciousness. we are different persons than when we started.

We experience this Consciousness in the natural world that surrounds our activity. We must recognize that this non-

Summary

human world is alive. Both philosophically and practically, we have to be concerned about the viability of this world. This is especially true for those outdoor athletes, those participating in sculling, cross country skiing, and cross country running. It was Thomas Berry who laid out the problem, the challenge that is before us, "The challenge of a planet severely damaged by an assault of unprecedented violence; a planet so toxic that rainfall is no longer the purest of waters, but has become sulfuric or nitric acid; a planet with rivers and seas severely polluted; a planet with its atmosphere diminished in its oxygen context and saturated with hydrocarbons; a planet with its continents impoverished in their capacity to support life because of the blacktopping and road building, erosion and strip mining." [106] Deliberately I once took a left turn out of the Craftsbury Sculling Center (The right turn is the usual exit method) and 45 minutes later we finally reached the blacktop. We were in close communion with Nature during this short drive.

We must be concerned as a community for the welfare of this Divine Earth and we must ensure that our athletes connect with their sacred surroundings as they man their Shells, run the countryside, and propel their skis over newly fallen snows. In

---

[106] Thomas Berry, *Evening Thoughts: reflecting on earth as a Sacred Community*, p.66.

The Quantum Sculler

this regard, we can learn much from the first nation peoples of the Americas and Asia.

British Sculler, F.S Kelly was a Diamond Sculls Winner and Olympic Gold Medalist. He recounts his connection to Nature at the height of the Henley Royal Regatta in 1910, "On an evening such as this was, all fragrance from the riverside gardens hangs over the surface of the water and one sculls Henley from one scent to another." [107] He was connecting to the environment through his sense of smell. Certainly, we can use our feel and sense of touch -- feel for the water and its power and sense of finger touch on the handles.

This connection to the non-human world is a far deeper and responsible objective for sport, than the usual promotion of winning. This requires a huge cultural shift in the thinking of the coach. His consciousness has to be enlarged. He has to be more concerned over the health of this beautiful earth. He has to move far beyond the simplistic world of winning and losing. He must see the Divine in our earth. We must become more attentive to simplicity, austerity, and light imprinting in our lives. We must be observant of our own being in this magnificent world. Our total coaching practice must reflect this, as we speak of the work process and not winning to our young people. For me, this has been a lifetime of shifting my goals from an empha-

---

[107] F. S. Kelly, *The Diaries of F.S. Kelly*

Summary

sis on winning, to goals that include communion, cooperation, and empathy. Sport becomes one of process, rather than a focus on the ends. It requires an expansive concern and feeling for a much larger situation beyond ourselves, beyond our human needs, and beyond the confines of our borders. Because it is more complex, our consciousness undergoes substantial growth.

According to contemporary physics, we are all connected, human and non-human. We must act with this in mind. This communion with the outside world is a missing element in our education. We gain access to our inner world through our awareness and study of the outer world. Both should be considered one, and are seamless. This study becomes an integral part of our mental and spiritual education. Mental Training is not simply an add-on, or a strategy, but is part of our everyday practice and existence. This study should begin for the young sculler with his initial step into the Shell. This education accepts the vagaries of the weather. They become challenges and learning situations and we function as one with the earth and the climate. We take on the mantle of gentle toughness and resiliency. All of this is part of our inner self and the education of the Self. This is viewing the world around us with a different set of eyes, nose and ears. Here in the Finger Lakes Region, we are so close to farms every day. They are a part of our deeper being. In larger cities, you have to seek out trees and small parcels of land. However, it begins with a much different intention and much different eyesight by each individual. We have to explore our deeper selves. We have to try to look beyond our modern conveniences and not get caught up in procuring the latest technological gadgets. We must consume less and leave a lighter footprint on this earth.

A final and necessary comment on great integral coaches goes to the late Allen Rosenberg. Allen spent an enormous amount of time on perfecting the movement patterns of his Olympic Champion Vesper crew in the 1963-64 season. He felt that you had to go slow before you could go fast. He always was careful that the crew was not overtrained. His methods included not only a well thought out training program that included weight training, speed and endurance water workouts from his readings of the great track coaches of the time, nutritional information for his athletes, mental training practices, technical/scientific rigging of shells, and the use of a coaching team with Detrich Rose. He was an innovator and educator. He didn't tell his people what to do, he explained and discussed what he was doing so that they understood. Al was using the Integral approach 50 years ago. Al was using the Integral approach 50 years ago.

Finally, the River Thames Scullers were free-wheeling explorers in the realm of body and water movement. They were evolutionaries. Their guidance was sought for a short time in England and America and then the University minds took over and the intuitive knowledge from these great performers of the waterways was lost. Consequently, we never speak of "watermanship". Instead the preoccupation of College Coaches may well be the GPS, the numbers, and the Erg score. We need these elementary statistics, but we also need to evaluate the Run of the Shell. We have lost our feel for how the Shell is "sliding or being pulled by a string." It is all about the quantitative rather than the qualitative. We have forgotten the lessons of the Pococks, Bert Haines, Bob Fitzpatrick, the Pearces. My goal with *The Quantum Sculler* is to resurrect the messages from these great scullers. They knew how shells moved best. With this approach, the study and practice of Sculling, again becomes an evolutionary path. It keeps opening up new possibilities, because it is an open-minded method. You are exploring much like they did on the water during every outing. Nothing is static. It is all in the future action. This is the challenge to keep your mind a beginner's mind, as promoted by Shunryu Suzuki. This forces one to be Integral in outlook and practice. Practice in Life and practice in Sculling. This way of life becomes all encompassing and thoroughly an evolution of one's thoughts. We become progressive, post-modern in our philosophy. You can feel it in your total being, as you explore this medium of how to move a slight Single Scull well. You are seeking as you observe. It is an exciting, spiritual endeavor that strikes and moves the heart of our being. It is a high form of Art.

The Quantum Sculler

There may be times when what is needed most is not so much a new discovery or a new idea, but a different 'slant'. I mean a comparatively slight adjustment in our way of looking at things and ideas on which attention is already fixed. [108]

This has been my intent throughout this book, a "slight adjustment" as to how we view the Stroke Cycle. *The Quantum Sculler* certainly takes the reader off of the normal "shipping lanes." I hope, in some small measure, that this objective has been achieved.

---

[108] Owen Barfield, *Saving the Appearances: A Study in Idolatry*, p.11.

Afterword

The Quantum Cycle

Beginning with the five movements of the release that look like one movement, to the ever changing motion of the trunk on the recovery, to the disappearing blade at the entry, to the combined, integral action of the arms, trunk, and legs on the drive, the stroke cycle is totally an expressed version of a Quantum state.

-Jimmy Joy

A few more thoughts from George Pocock that reinforce that which has been stated earlier in the text:

"When the blades catch the water for a stroke and the blades have to turn from the horizontal, do not for a moment think that the wrists do it all. It is the same principle as when the blades leave the water -- let the water do it, turn the wrists slightly, and relax the grip. The water will square the blades if given a chance. Remember the water is a constant; use it. Again the scull handles will turn a few degrees in the relaxed hand. As the stroke is coming through, never grip the scull handle tightly, but relax the grip and more or less make hooks of the hands. Gripping tires the forearms and is apt to cramp the muscles." [109]

Reading Pocock and Frank Cunningham on the skill of Bert Haines, I come away with the feeling of how important the accuracy, fineness, and timing of the power is for "running" the shell. This is true in the power of weight application of weight lifters as well. You can see their coordination and timing expressed to the utmost. I witnessed this on two occasions comparing the movements of young athletes with their weight training coaches. The coaches were much more fluid and coordinated. For this reason, Freshman Coach Rusty Callow at the University of Washington had an older George Pocock get into his shell and demonstrate his movements to his crews.

This is the state, the art, the shell run that we are trying to achieve. This is the elusive element in our coaching and the athlete's doing. It goes beyond, well beyond, the actual strength of the crew, its size, and its erg numbers. Just how effective are the athletes in achieving Pocock's Harmony, Balance, and Rhythm, the ingredients necessary for achieving fluid, effortless shell run. These are the ingredients of all great sculler's such as Ned Hanlan, Ernest Barry, Jack Kelly Sr., Robert Pearce, Joe Burk, Dick

---

[109] *Memories* by George Yeoman Pocock

Afterword

and George Pocock, Bert Haines, Vyacheslav Petti Karpineen, and Thomas Lange.

Appendix - Movement Training Drills

Introduction

Drills are the backbone of the Training Program. This is where the Sculler touches base with his Movement Patterns. The objective of each drill is to move ever closer to perfection of specific Movement involved. So, concentration on the task must be extremely high. Although the drill only covers a part of the stroke, the Sculler must keep in mind, the Wholeness of the Movement. With this approach, we are moving toward achieving the Flow State. The Sculler must have a thorough understanding of why he is doing a particular drill. So each drill has a clear purpose. In turn, the coach must have a high degree of concentration as well. Each drill must be executed properly and the coach must monitor the quality of the completed Movement. The athlete has to be aware of the quality of each Movement, as well. So drills assist with the development of concentration levels of both Sculler and Coach.

Select a quiet space of water of 1,500 to 2,000 meters and do multiple repetitions in this restricted space to keep intensity high. Relief for the athlete comes in turning the Shell. The coach should maintain close attention to detail and be very demanding, stopping the Shell frequently to correct Movements. This practice should be done once a week during the performance

Appendix - Movement Training Drills

season. During the preseason, this practice can be done 2 to 3 times a week. This is an excellent way to improve fluid Shell Run, so these intensity sessions are done throughout the year.

Drills can be used in three ways, as a warm-up, as a warm-down, and as a regular training mode. Slow Motion Rowing increases Awareness and Sensitivity.

Posture

Sit with an erect spine with even pressure on both buttocks. Hold the Sculling handles with an even pressure. Place even pressure on the footplates. Head is up and looking past the stern of the Shell. Be aware of the contribution of your peripheral vision. It is an excellent way to remain in touch with the riverbank. Fingers have a very light hold of the handles.

Release

- Tapping Drill to a pause at 1/2 blade out, for timing.
- One hand rowing and single side sculling.
- One stroke runs with a pause at 3" from the body, or at one-quarter slide.
- Wide grip rowing and sculling.
- Change of speed rowing (controlled by the stroke man).
- One-quarter slide back-end. With no trunk, and with trunk.

- One-quarter slide back-end. Quick to very quick and spirited. Lots of fun at a rate of 62 strokes per minute.

Follow-Through
- One stroke runs from hands position. Hands pause at 3 - 6" away from the body.
- 1-3-5 strokes drill with a pause at the hands or one-quarter slide positions.
- Single stroke pulls from entry to one-quarter slide forward, pause, reset at full-slide, pause, then pull.

Recovery
- Blade placements moving from 0 slide to three-quarter slide starting points.
- One stroke runs with a pause at hands position, 6" away from the body.
- Slow motion feathering. Rowing using full-slide. Blade eventually can be carried off the water as balance improves.
- On the Ergometer or in tank, move body up and down the slide on the coach's command. Starting at 0, to one-quarter, one-half, three-quarter, full, three-quarter, one-half, one-quarter, and 0 slide positions. This is a great drill for group timing.

Appendix - Movement Training Drills

- Simulation Exercise. With one foot on bench and opposite leg straight to begin, then swing trunk forward bending the leg.

Entry

- Place your hand in front of you palm up. Then let the little finger lead the hand downward simulating the drop of the blade.
- Sitting at three-quarter slide, let the blade drop in from the horizontal. The lower edge of the blade takes a curvilinear path to the water resting at blade width depth.
- Blade set in starting from three-quarter, one-half, one-quarter, 0 slide position and then moving to full-slide. This is easy to more difficult for timing
- Blade set in and grips the water.
- One stroke pulls.
- One-quarter slide rowing, front-end.
- One stroke pull runs with a pause at one-half or three-quarter slide on the Recovery.
- One-quarter slide back-end, quick hands out of bow to facilitate Entry action.
- Slow Motion Sculling, concentrating on "lower edge rowing".
- Placement drills from 0 slide with blade placed at 3/4, 1/2, 1/4 covered.

Drive

- One stroke pulls with blade at blade-depth, feel for uniform pressure on blade face throughout the whole drive and relate body action to the pressure on the blade face.
- Blade set in and pulls starting from three-quarter slide position.
- One-half slide middle with no trunk action. With arms and without arms engaged.
- Pulls with blade slightly pitched in water for feel (internal rigging).
- Pull hard and harder (3 stroke sequence of hard, harder, light). This is a simulation of your approach to racing with first-half hard and second-half harder. Bring the above strategy down to a single stroke – first, half-hard and second, half- harder stroke, followed by a light stroke.

Simulation Exercises

Performed on the Ergometer without and with the oar handle. The Stroke Cycle is broken down into parts, and repeated practice is performed to achieve mastery with great results for timing and balance. These exercises were used at Yale in the late 60's and early 70's with good results.

Appendix - Movement Training Drills

Drills for Novices

- Sit at 0 slide and use trunk and arms only. Check posture.
- Sit at 0 slide. Check hand levels and use one-quarter slide rowing. Check posture.
- Sit at 0 slide and do the Tapping Drill. Check posture.
- Do single stroke pulls from one-half slide to a pause at 6" off the body position.
- Do single-side sculling.

Advanced Scullers Drills

- The three-pause drill. Pause at 3" off the trunk, pause at three-quarter slide, and pause with blade covered at full-slide.
- One-quarter slide front-end sculling.
- One-quarter slide back-end sculling.
- One-half slide middle sculling with and without arms, with and without trunk engaged.
- Start at full-slide with blades three-quarters covered. Scull slowly. Then go to one-half blade covered. And, finally to one-quarter blade covered.
- Slow Motion with flat wrists at the Release.
- Sit at three-quarter slide and do a simple rhythmic drop and slight pull at full-reach.

The Quantum Sculler

- One-half and three-quarter slide rowing. With arms and no arms; trunk and no trunk movements.
- "Back chaining" from three-quarter slide or full slide, then release and move back to three-quarter slide position. When you get more skilled, you can have the blade off the water throughout the drill.

Bibliography

Barfield, Owen, *Saving the Appearances: A Study in Idolatry*
Berry, Thomas, *The Sacred Universe*
Berry, Wendell, *Harlan Hubbard*
Bohm, David, *On Dialogue*; *On Creativity*
Bohm, David and Peat, F. David, *Science, Order, and Creativity*; *Unfolding Meaning*; *Wholeness and the Implicate Order.*
Deck, John, N, *Nature, Contemplation, and the One: A study in the Philosophy of Plotinus.*
Doidge, Norman, M.D. *The Brain's Way of Healing*
Eknath, Easwaran, *Passage Meditation: Bringing the Deep Wisdom of the Heart into Daily Life*; *Strength in the Storm: Transform Stress, Live in Balance and Find Peace of Mind*; *Take your Time*; *The Upanishads*
Feldenkrais, Moshe, *Awareness Through Movement*; *The Potent Self*
Feuerstein, Georg, *Structures of Consciousness*
Ford, Scott, *Welcome to the Zone: Peak Performance Redefined*
Fox, Matthew, *Meister Eckhart*
Gebser, Jean, *The Ever-Present Origin*
Goswani, Amit, *Quantum Creativity*
Hadot, Pierre, *The Inner Citadel: The Meditations of Marcus Aurelius*
Herberger, Ernst, *The GDR Text of Oarsmanship*
Hicks, C. Scot and David V., *The Emperor's Handbook*

Bibliography

Honore, Carl, *In Praise of Slowness*
Hubbard, Harlan, *Payne Hollow*
Johnson, Will, *The Posture of Meditation*
Krishnamurti, J., *Freedom from the Known*
Krishnamurti, J., and Bohm, David, *The Limits of Thought; The Ending of Time*
Kumar, Satish, *You are Therefore I Am; Spiritual Compass: The Three Qualities of Life*
Nadolny, Sten, *The Discovery of Slowness*
Newell, George, *Ready All! George Yeoman Pocock and Crew Racing*
Peat, F. David, Infinite Potential: *The Life and Times of David Bohm*
Phipps, Carter, *Evolutionaries: Unlocking the Spiritual and Cultural Potential of Science's Greatest Idea*
Pocock, George Yeoman, *Memories*
Richards, Mary Caroline, *Centering in Poetry, Pottery, and Prose*.
Sherrington, Sir Charles, *Man on His Nature*.
Talbot, Michael, *Beyond the Quantum; The Holographic Universe; Mysticism and the New Physics*
Tallis, Raymond, *Aping Mankind: Neuromanis, Darwinitis and the Misrepresentation of Humanity*.
Tesla, Nikola, *The Nikola Tesla Treasury*.
Vaughan-Lee, Llewlleyn, *Reclaiming the Feminine Mystery of Creation*
Wilber, Ken, ed., *The Holographic Paradigm*

Acknowledgements

The contributions to this little book came from various people including Scott Ford, Paul Fuchs, Steve Haase, Lindsey Hochman, Giusseppe Lund, Dennis Fronheiser, Tim Giarrusso, Nich Lee Parker, Barry Robbins, Paul Thompson, Mike Wagner, Amy Wettergreen Smack, and Art Wilmarth. I am especially appreciative of Vince Reynolds's many, many emails to me outlining his experiments in the scull with the Quantum approach. He is a true believer.

I thank David Meggyesy for his fine Introduction. David is a convert to sculling from NFL football.

My appreciation goes to Rebecca Craies for her support, encouragement, and for being instrumental in having this book published as a kindle edition through *Rowperfect, UK*.

I value the extensive editing by my former Yale 150 student/athlete-rowers, Tom Weil and Jon VanAmringe, former Naval Academy Lightweight Crew head coach. Tom is the world's leading collector of rowing art and the promoter/lecturer of the origin of rowing coming from work rather than from play. They have done a wonderful job. I am so fortunate to have them. Both have experienced previous editing with *The Mind's Eye* and *Hanlan's Spirit*.

I would like to acknowledge Haley Sive, for her outstanding design of our cover, many thanks Haley.

Finally, I owe a great deal of thanks to Mike Wagner, Haley, and Jon VanAmringe for their large efforts to put the finishing touches to the book and get it published.

About the Author

Jimmy Joy began sculling at the age of 15 and has coached rowing for more than 35 years in both Canada and the USA. He is also the founder of the acclaimed Joy of Sculling Coaches Conference that annually for 24 years has provided an environment to foster the teaching of integral coaching techniques and philosophy. At Joy of Sculling, coaches from throughout North America and internationally, can share and learn from each other.

A native of St. Catherines, Ontario, he was fortunate there to have a Master Sculling Coach in Bob Fitzpatrick. "Fitz" earlier coached the undefeated Olympic and World Champion sculler, Bobby Pearce. From his 15-year experience with Fitzpatrick as mentor, Joy developed an eclectic and highly effective sculling technique, which includes elements of Orthodoxy, Fairbairn and Pearce. Jimmy went on to successfully coach at the University of Western Ontario, MIT, Yale, Wesleyan, and Hobart William Smith. He also taught academic courses at both Wesleyan and Hobart on the psychology and philosophical nature of sport.

During the 1980s, Jimmy served as Technical Director for Rowing Canada. His initiatives there included the Apprenticeship Program, small boat clinics, speed order trials, physiological testing, bi-monthly Coaches' Notes and an annual National Rowing Coaches' Conference. The program was very successful with the Canadian crews winning more than 60 medals at various international competitions. In 1989, he became Head Rowing Coach at Hobart William Smith. There he employed a "holistic" coaching approach that in a few short years developed a nationally recognized collegiate rowing program.

Jimmy's reach in coaching and rowing is extensive. He co-founded the Craftsbury Sculling Camp that continues to have a positive impact on competitive and recreational sculling in America and beyond. He also continues to teach at Black Bear Sculling.

The Quantum Sculler is his third book, following *The Mind's Eye: The Evolution of the Athletes' Skills and Consciousness* and *Hanlan's Spirit: Training for Flow*. In these books, Jimmy has put forth, for coaches, rowers and others to experience, his years of research on Integral Coaching, Flow, Mental Training for coaches and the functional athlete, as well as the converging process of Skills and Consciousness.

Jimmy and his wife Cele currently reside in Geneva, NY. He continues his sculling on the Cayuga-Seneca Canal.

www.ingramcontent.com/pod-product-compliance
Lightning Source LLC
Chambersburg PA
CBHW020923090426
42736CB00010B/1021